# DiRTY
## CHRiSTiANiTY

# DiRTY
## CHRiSTiANiTY

we've left something out of the gospel

By

Warren H. Stewart, Jr.

authorHOUSE®

AuthorHouse™
1663 Liberty Drive
Bloomington, IN 47403
www.authorhouse.com
Phone: 1-800-839-8640

Published by AuthorHouse    11/06/2012

ISBN: 978-1-4772-7645-7 (sc)
ISBN: 978-1-4772-7643-3 (hc)
ISBN: 978-1-4772-7644-0 (e)

Library of Congress Control Number: 2012918371

Cover Design: BIGWO Designs
Author Photo: Mary Jordan
First Edition 2012
Published by Warren H. Stewart, Jr.
www.dirtychristianity.com

# TABLE OF CONTENTS

Father, I thank You for YOUR LOVE, GRACE, MERCY, and FORGIVENESS You give to me everyday. Thank You for always being near to me. Thank You for Your HOLINESS. Your LOVE is set apart from everyone else. Your GOODNESS humbles me to repentance. Thank you for always loving me despite me. You are My God, My Savior, and My Comforter. You are the Lover of my soul and the Forgiver of my sins. I LOVE YOU DADDY!

# DEDICATIONS

This book is dedicated to my beautiful and loving wife Chrystal. You are such an inspiration to me through the Love, Grace, and Goodness of God. Thank you for trusting God in me to lead our family and for being my partner in life and ministry. I'm so glad I don't have to take this journey alone. Our Father has so much in store for us and I can't wait to experience the fullness of God with you. You are my good thing!
I LOVE YOU BABY!

To our children Josiah, Micaiah, and Kaira. Daddy loves you with all of his heart. Thank you for always loving me unconditionally. I am thankful to have such understanding children who love the Lord at your ages and are on this journey with Mommy and Daddy. I can't wait to see what our Daddy has destined you to become. We are leaving a legacy for you.

To Church of The Remnant, I am humbled and honored to serve as your pastor. You all have heard these messages, themes, and stories throughout the years and I am grateful that you all are growing as Disciples of Christ and Bereans of His Word. #serveoneanother #loveoneanother #acts2ministry #chURch #tellyourstory

As sinful people we are NOT loved by God because we are beautiful; rather we are beautiful because we are loved by God. The more we surrender and absorb His love for us, the more vulnerable and honest we can be about our TRUE selves, especially the weak, needy, broken and angry parts of ourselves.

—Dr. Steven and Celestia Tracy

# PREFACE

The church and modern Christianity has lost its authenticity! No one wants to tell their "dirty" stories of redemption anymore. We live in a broken world, full of fallen people who act as if they have no flaws once they have come to Jesus. There is not one perfect human being but Jesus Christ. Yet, Christians have hid behind the religious fallacy that we have to mask the past and act like we have been spotless since birth. People need to know that *His*tory changed our story.

We hide behind church attire, church jargon, multi-site church campuses, social cliques in the church, and brag about being in the ministry for so many odd years. While all this looks good externally, it is intimidating at times to the common unbeliever or sinner. We have focused so much on the edifice and external extremities of the church in American Christianity that we lose focus that our hearts are the very thing Jesus came to change.

Most "unchurched" or "unbelievers" as we call them, feel unworthy to even come to God because of how Christians have portrayed Jesus. Why is this? It is not that God's loving arms are not open; it's that a vast majority of Christian's arms are folded and their eyes are crossed, looking down upon people that don't fit into our Christian norm.

As Christians we are afraid to get "dirty." We are afraid of people's brokenness. We are afraid to deal with pain. We are afraid to deal with the issues Jesus came to comfort. We are afraid to really be like Jesus! We have prejudice for who we think is worthy of the love and grace of God. We judge, not racially but spiritually who should be at "our" church or not. And in my estimation some churches still do judge racially.

Were we not that "dirty" sinner before we found grace? Were we not the one who was in desperate need of saving? Were we not the one who felt unworthy to be loved by the God of the universe? Are we still not one who struggles with sin every now and then after coming to Jesus? So why have we forgotten our redemption story? Why are we afraid to reflect on where God brought us from?

I challenge you to examine your life and find that one common factor that sinners, the unchurched, unbelievers or whatever we want to label them will want to discover. The gospel of Jesus Christ is real and relevant because they will hear how our lives were changed forever because of an encounter with the heavenly Father who adopted us as sons and daughters.

There is one particular story in the Bible that the church rarely pauses to reflect on in preaching the gospel. And for many years I have wrestled with why we neglected such an important message, which Jesus said we should include in the gospel. It is the story of Mary of Bethany who anointed Jesus for His burial. However, Jesus is not just one-dimensional, only pointing out the significant anointing. I was pricked in my heart to discover that this woman's story of brokenness and boldness all in one scene is recorded in every gospel account. I see another page of her story that we have overlooked biblically and practically in our personal lives when sharing the gospel. True biblical interpretation is effective only after application. So if we are not applying the gospel message intertwined with our stories of redemption, has it truly gripped our hearts?

In my opinion, the modern church and "American Christianity" is far from preaching the gospel of Jesus Christ as Jesus commissioned His Disciples. What I see is pretext preaching, topical teaching, and inspiring intellectual messages that are causing people to feel good, but where is the power of the gospel to change lives in truth and love? Christians are too apathetic and are focused on me and mine and not the lost and broken. There is a shallow selfish seeking of God for material satisfaction rather than for souls that need saving and then equating the amounts we are blessed with to authentic faith. This is not a universal gospel.

When someone was "dirty" in the religious culture in Jesus' time, they were never afraid to come to Jesus, nor was He afraid to become "dirty" because of their sin. They did not and were not allowed to go to the temple or synagogue because they were labeled outcasts by the laws and extra religious practices of the Pharisees, Sadducees and religious authorities. But they came to Jesus! Do sinners feel that you are approachable? If Jesus could stoop down to sinners, eat with sinners, and talk to sinners, then why have we not followed the Master Teacher? There is a dying world of people who need this Jesus that we claim to believe in, but don't fully display in character. So who is the true unbeliever? Those in the church or outside of the church?

This is a book of redemptive power to be like Jesus Christ, without the boundaries of religion that keep people stiff-necked and selective with the gospel. This book is to wake Christians up and make sinners aware that they have a right to search for authentic Christianity. This book is a voice crying out for those who are weeping in shame, guilt, regret and brokenness and pointing them to a God who desperately loves them and wants to make them whole through His grace, but using our arms as the first contact of the love of God.

As a purposed illustration, even the white book cover and pages will get "dirty," but the content will remain pure. This is the story of our lives. We may be in these earthen broken vessels, but our treasure resides in our Relationship with our Redeemer who has purified us with His Word. The "i" dotted with the blood splatter signifies that Christ has dotted every "i" and crossed the "t" on Calvary's cross despising the shame covering us and giving us the confidence to share our redemption stories because of His work to save us and not of ourselves.

So we can't judge a "dirty" book by its cover until we read and discover the content on the inside.

We will be going through many Scriptural texts and references because the Word of God is our source of authority for living as Believers. The reason for many Scriptures being quoted in full or what would seem lengthy is to forego any assumption that any Christian or non-Christian will open their Bible while reading this book. It is my prayer that someone who may not own a Bible or who hasn't read Scripture lately may be transformed because God's Word is infused throughout this literary text (2 Timothy 3:16-17).

*Dirty Christianity* will challenge you on a prescriptive scriptural journey of transparency and authenticity to tell your redemption story and make the gospel relevant to those who desperately need the loving embrace of God the Father, the amazing grace through Jesus Christ and the refreshing filling of the Holy Spirit. In turn, this gospel that has changed your life just may grip you again.

"If you believe what you like in the gospels, and reject what you don't like, it is not the gospel you believe, but yourself."—Saint Augustine

# CHAPTER 1

## THE GOSPEL

Growing up in the Baptist church I often heard the gospel preached at the close or the celebration part of the message. My dad was my pastor so I heard it almost every week. If you can imagine this in a black Baptist preacher's tone of voice, I'm getting ready to close . . . "Jesus died on Friday! He was buried . . . in a borrowed tomb! Stayed there all day Saturday! But early! Y'all didn't hear me . . . I said early Sunday morning! Heh! He got up with all power in His hands!" Of course that's when the church would go wild and crazy. It brings great joy to even write and reflect on these moments, but as I grew older I discovered that the gospel was more than just the celebration part of church or the end of a sermon. It is the entire reason we have church.

In 1 Corinthians 15:1-8 (NASB) we have the gospel according to Scripture:

> Now I make known to you, brethren, the gospel which I preached to you, which also you received, in which also you stand, by which also you are saved, if you hold fast the word

which I preached to you, unless you believed in vain. For I delivered to you as of first importance what I also received, that Christ died for our sins according to the Scriptures, and that He was buried, and that He was raised on the third day according to the Scriptures, and that He appeared to Cephas, then to the twelve. After that He appeared to more than five hundred brethren at one time, most of whom remain until now, but some have fallen asleep; then He appeared to James, then to all the apostles; and last of all, as to one untimely born, He appeared to me also.

Paul lays the foundation of the gospel very sound theologically, but how is this relevant to someone outside of church? The reality is some people outside of church respect God in a manner that Christians sometimes don't. Unbelievers won't come to church because of the sin in their lives and feel they need to clean themselves up before coming to God. They feel they need to know enough Scripture or pray more. They feel afraid that the church will burn up if they walk in. Why do they feel this way?

What I love about 1 Corinthians 15 is the fact that Jesus didn't just resurrect and go to heaven, but He appeared to those that believed, those who doubted and Saul who was persecuting the church (Acts 9:1-31).

Jesus is no respecter of persons and wants to give the most undeserved person the privilege of being in a relationship with Him through the grace of God.

Here's the question, Is He appearing through us? Colossians 3:27b (NASB), says "it is Christ in us the hope of glory." We must offer hope to people who feel unworthy to come to "our church." We must understand that we are the church, not the building! We need to walk and talk with people and appear to them as Jesus did to us.

## iNSPiRED BY A TRUE STORY

The harsh reality is some of us do not even know how to evangelize or witness in the sense of "old school" evangelism. We focus more on getting membership rather than discipleship, which is a major problem in American Christianity. It's big business now more than Kingdom business. Many Christians in church today do not know how to articulate the gospel message, but we know how to tell our story don't we? We need to know how to say who we were before Jesus, who we are once we encountered Jesus and who we still are with Jesus. The people that Jesus encountered throughout the Bible were all INSPIRED BY A TRUE STORY.

The crux of our faith resides on the fact not just that He got up early Sunday morning (Resurrected) and the tomb is empty, but that He appeared to over 500 people. By these appearances others became instant believers because Jesus was a Man of truth. People need to hear about your encounter with Jesus that changed your life forever. And I will go on to say you should still be having great encounters with the Holy Spirit that are fresh and fill you to live a godly life for the glory of God alone.

The gospel is simply good news. Our lives before Jesus sucked! We were born into sin, we would never have enough animals to sacrifice to make atonement for our sins and we were bound for hell and deserved it. That's the bad news. Some of us have not come to grips yet with the fact that we didn't save ourselves through religion or good works. This is why many people outside of church do not come in or have left the church because they never feel like they could ever be good enough for God. When were we ever good enough?

> But we are all like an unclean *thing*, And all our righteousnesses *are* like filthy rags; We all fade as a leaf, And our iniquities, like the wind, Have taken us away.
>
> —Isaiah 64:6 NKJV

And do not enter into judgment with Your servant, For in Your sight no man living is righteous.

—Psalm 143:2 NASB

What then? Are we better than they? Not at all; for we have already charged that both Jews and Greeks are all under sin; as it is written, "THERE IS NONE RIGHTEOUS, NOT EVEN ONE;"

—Romans 3:9-10 NASB

And Jesus said to him, "Why do you call Me good? No one is good except God alone."

—Mark 10:18 NASB

but God has chosen the foolish things of the world to shame the wise, and God has chosen the weak things of the world to shame the things which are strong, and the base things of the world and the despised God has chosen, the things that are not, so that He may nullify the things that are, so that no man may boast before God. But by His doing you are in Christ Jesus, who became to us wisdom from God, and righteousness and sanctification, and redemption, so that, just as it is written, "LET HIM WHO BOASTS, BOAST IN THE LORD."

—1 Corinthians 1:27-31 NASB

We must say to every sinner we didn't do anything to save ourselves. We received a free gift of Salvation.

But God, being rich in mercy, because of His great love with which He loved us, even when we were dead in our transgressions, made us alive together with Christ (by grace you have been saved), and raised us up with Him, and seated us with Him in the heavenly *places* in Christ Jesus, so that in the ages to come He might show the surpassing riches of His grace in kindness toward us in Christ Jesus. **For by grace you have been saved through faith; and that not of yourselves, *it is* the gift of God; not as a result of works, so that no one may boast.** For we are His workmanship, created in Christ Jesus for good works, which God prepared beforehand so that we would walk in them.

—Ephesians 2:4-10 NASB

We were separated from God by sin brought into the world by Adam. We as Jews or Gentiles could not live up to the 613 Old Testament Commandments, let alone the 10. This is why God sent Jesus to be the perfect innocent sacrifice for the sins of all mankind when we were guilty. This is the good news:

Therefore, having been justified by faith, we have peace with God through our Lord Jesus Christ, through whom also we have obtained our introduction by faith into this grace in which we stand; and we exult in hope of the glory of God. And not only this, but we also exult in our tribulations, knowing that tribulation brings about perseverance; and perseverance, proven character; and proven character, hope; and hope does not disappoint, because the love of God has been poured out within our hearts through the Holy Spirit who was given to us. For while we were still helpless, at the right time Christ died for the ungodly. For one will hardly die for a righteous man; though perhaps for the good man someone would dare even to die. But God demonstrates His own love toward us, in that while we were yet sinners, Christ died for us. Much more then, having now been justified by His blood, we shall be saved from the wrath *of God* through Him. For if while we were enemies we were reconciled to God through the death of His Son, much more, having been reconciled, we shall be saved by His life. And not only this, but we also exult in God through our Lord Jesus Christ, through whom we have now received the reconciliation. Therefore, just as through one man sin entered into the world, and death through sin, and so death spread to all men, because all sinned—for until the Law sin was in the world, but sin is not imputed when there is no law. Nevertheless death reigned from Adam until Moses, even over those who had not sinned in the likeness of the offense of Adam, who is a type of Him who was to come. But the free gift is not like the transgression. For if by the transgression of the one the many died, much more did the grace of God and the gift by the grace of the one Man, Jesus Christ, abound to the many. The gift is not like *that which came* through the one who sinned; for on the one hand the judgment *arose* from one *transgression* resulting in condemnation, but on the other hand the free gift *arose* from many transgressions resulting in justification. For if by the transgression of the one, death reigned through the one, much more those who receive the abundance of grace and of the gift of righteousness will reign in life through the One, Jesus Christ. So then as through one transgression there resulted condemnation to all men, even so through one act of righteousness there resulted justification of life to all men. For as through the one man's disobedience the many were made sinners, even so through the obedience of the One the many will be made righteous. The Law came in so that the transgression would increase; but where sin increased, grace abounded all the more, so that, as sin reigned in death, even so grace would reign through righteousness to eternal life through Jesus Christ our Lord.

—Romans 5:1-21 NASB


He who knew no sin became sin (DIRTY) for those who believe so they would not have to feel the wrath of God. Jesus lived a perfect life for us and fulfilled ALL of God's commands so that we might be saved.

He made Him who knew no sin *to be* sin on our behalf, so that we might become the righteousness of God in Him.

—1 Corinthians 5:21 NASB

Isaiah 53:1-12 (NKJV)

"Who has believed our report?
And to whom has the arm of the LORD been revealed?
For He shall grow up before Him as a tender plant,
And as a root out of dry ground.

He has no form or comeliness;
And when we see Him,
*There is* no beauty that we should desire Him.
He is despised and rejected by men,
A Man of sorrows and acquainted with grief.
And we hid, as it were, *our* faces from Him;
He was despised, and we did not esteem Him.
Surely He has borne our griefs
And carried our sorrows;
Yet we esteemed Him stricken,
Smitten by God, and afflicted.
But He *was* wounded for our transgressions,
*He was* bruised for our iniquities;
The chastisement for our peace *was* upon Him,
And by His stripes we are healed.
All we like sheep have gone astray;
We have turned, every one, to his own way;
And the LORD has laid on Him the iniquity of us all.

He was oppressed and He was afflicted,
Yet He opened not His mouth;
He was led as a lamb to the slaughter,
And as a sheep before its shearers is silent,
So He opened not His mouth.
He was taken from prison and from judgment,
And who will declare His generation?
For He was cut off from the land of the living;
For the transgressions of My people He was stricken.
And they made His grave with the wicked—
But with the rich at His death,

Because He had done no violence,
Nor *was any* deceit in His mouth.

Yet it pleased the LORD to bruise Him;
He has put *Him* to grief.
When You make His soul an offering for sin,
He shall see *His* seed, He shall prolong *His* days,
And the pleasure of the LORD shall prosper in His hand.
He shall see the labor of His soul, *and* be satisfied.
By His knowledge My righteous Servant shall justify many,
For He shall bear their iniquities."

Isaiah 53 is the prophecy of how the servant Messiah would be slighted, suffer, submit, and satisfy the requirements for our salvation. He was rejected, spit on, punched, stripped naked, flogged, ridiculed, and mocked. His beard was plucked out, He was falsely accused, crucified, died and rose again; all so that we who believe in Him could never be separated from God by sin ever again. Separation from God is truly death and God did not want us to ever experience it because He loves us. God being holy, merciful, and just had to judge sin and chose to put our penalty on His only begotten Son.

When we believe by faith alone in Christ alone, the work of Jesus' life, death, and resurrection is applied to us and we are regenerated by the Holy Spirit of God and become His children. At this point we are new creations (2 Corinthians 5:17) and the old has passed away. Jesus says,

> "Truly, truly, I say to you, he who hears My word, and believes Him who sent Me, has eternal life, and does not come into judgment, but has passed out of death into life."
>
> —John 5:24 NASB

This is the gospel that has caused us to be saved. WE WERE SAVED BY GOD, FROM GOD, FOR GOD! And there is nothing we can do to break the seal of our salvation (Ephesians 1:13). WE MUST BE ABLE TO ARTICULATE THE GOSPEL, THE BAD NEWS AND THE GOOD NEWS!

> In Him, you also, after listening to the message of truth, the gospel of your salvation—having also believed, you were sealed in Him with the Holy Spirit of promise,
>
> —Ephesians 1:13 NASB

Scripturally and theologically we can articulate and argue the tenants of the doctrine of Soteriology (the study of salvation), but as I stated earlier, we must include our relevant redemption stories in the gospel message.

If you are reading this for the first time and have realized you have not believed the gospel by faith alone in Christ alone, even if you have been in church for many years and claimed to be a Christian, you can confess and believe in Him and receive the free GIFT of salvation right now. Sincerely ask God to save you, forgive you for your sins, thank Him for it and ask the Holy Spirit to lead and guide you in His Word and Truth so that you may know God intimately and have a fruitful relationship with Him all the days of your life. After doing so, you are now His child and He is your Father. Follow Him!

> But what does it say? "The word is near you, in your mouth and in your heart"—that is, the word of faith which we are preaching, that if you confess with your mouth Jesus as Lord, and believe in your heart that God raised Him from the dead, you will be saved; for with the heart a person believes, resulting in righteousness, and with the mouth he confesses, resulting in salvation. For the Scripture says, "Whoever believes in Him will not be disappointed." For there is no distinction between Jew and Greek; for the same Lord is Lord of all, abounding in riches for all who call

on Him; for "Whoever will call on the name of the Lord will be saved."

—Romans 10:8-13 NASB

This is eternal life, that they may know You, the only true God, and Jesus Christ whom You have sent.

—John 17:3 NASB

# CHAPTER 2

## HOW DiRTY WERE YOU?

There is a childhood saying, "God made dirt and dirt don't hurt." God also made us from dirt and that is the origin of mankind, but dirt in context of our past is often connected to shame, hurt, regret, abuse, neglect, and guilt. So that dirt still does hurt some.

Many people are challenged in this area of their past and many Christians do not want you to know who they used to be. HOW DIRTY WERE YOU? When was the last time you shared your testimony? When was the last time you just broke out in "a praise" after having a flashback of the old you and thanked God that you are not the same person you used to be? Go ahead right now if you haven't done it in awhile . . .

Remember, I grew up in the church all my life, I repeat, all my life and we used to have testimony service back in the day. People would share what the Lord had done in their lives during a worship service and tell of God's goodness despite their downfalls. Some would be transparent, some would blame the devil or speak of his attacks on them, and some would share things like they were "saved all their life." And no they were not speaking about election. I found this "saved all your life" statement to be odd, as I came to understand salvation in later years. Now, I knew I was in church all my life, but did not accept Jesus until I was ten years old. So why did some of these people want to portray themselves as perfect in front of the church?

At the age of ten I had no real "dirt" to testify about. In retrospect, I could say I stole small toys and lied to my parents, but no real juicy story to share during testimony service. Now I am not condoning going into the world and rolling with the pigs to get dirty just so we can have more sins forgiven, but I will explain how someone thought this was supposed to be the case for a Christian's testimony. Some may have a PG rated testimony and others may have an XXX rated one, but the bottom line is Jesus wipes ALL the sin away through repentance.

## DiRTY TESTiMONiES

We are very intentional about discipleship training at Church of The Remnant, and in our curriculum we give a model for sharing your testimony. I told the church one Tuesday night at discipleship training, before we go out among strangers let's get comfortable in sharing with the body of believers. They had two weeks to prepare. We lost half the class! For those who stayed, I found some interesting perspectives on what they thought testimonies were.

One said she thought she had to go get a testimony to have one. In other words, she assumed she had to live an ungodly life through sex, drugs, and clubbing in order to have a "certified" testimony. I was floored by hearing this. Others told their story for the first time and had never revealed their dark past to anyone. Another had so much fear of people judging her that she almost did not want to speak. She stood and just cried her way through the whole thing. There was so much victory in this for her. By giving her testimony God freed her from things that were haunting her and she is one of the most beloved members we have. God even healed her from her sleep apnea that night! She got free from the fear of people's opinions.

For those that left the class and even the church, it scared them away to have to reveal how "dirty" they used to be. We discovered that some people still live in the shame of their past and have not been freed from regret. Some were afraid of what people may have thought of them. We did not do this to expose anyone's "dirt" it was simply a discipleship exercise that pointed to a deeper reality for some, shame.

## PRODiGAL SON

In Luke 15, we have the parables of the lost and found coin, the lost and found sheep, and the lost and found son. The bigger picture of these parables is the Love of God and His pursuit after sinners. The parables climaxed with the prodigal son, the loving father, and the prideful son. The younger son told his father he was dead to him by asking for his inheritance before his father's death. Then he squanders his money through loose living and ends up in a disgusting place spiritually, mentally, and physically, wallowing with filthy pigs. And yet he comes to himself by eating from the carob tree, which is a tree that points to what Israel would be reduced to eat in order to turn back to God in repentance (Ederskein).

> And He said, "A man had two sons. The younger of them said to his father, 'Father, give me the share of the estate that falls to me.' So he divided his wealth between them. And

not many days later, the younger son gathered everything together and went on a journey into a distant country, and there he squandered his estate with loose living. Now when he had spent everything, a severe famine occurred in that country, and he began to be impoverished. So he went and hired himself out to one of the citizens of that country, and he sent him into his fields to feed swine. And he would have gladly filled his stomach with the pods that the swine were eating, and no one was giving *anything* to him. But when he came to his senses, he said, 'How many of my father's hired men have more than enough bread, but I am dying here with hunger! I will get up and go to my father, and will say to him, 'Father, I have sinned against heaven, and in your sight; I am no longer worthy to be called your son; make me as one of your hired men.' So he got up and came to his father. But while he was still a long way off, his father saw him and felt compassion *for him,* and ran and embraced him and kissed him. And the son said to him, 'Father, I have sinned against heaven and in your sight; I am no longer worthy to be called your son.' But the father said to his slaves, 'Quickly bring out the best robe and put it on him, and put a ring on his hand and sandals on his feet; and bring the fattened calf, kill it, and let us eat and celebrate; for this son of mine was dead and has come to life again; he was lost and has been found.' And they began to celebrate."

—Luke 15:11-24 NASB

## LOVE WiLL MAKE YOU LiVE AGAiN

In verse 18, before the prodigal son comes home he begins to rehearse his repentance or his testimony saying to himself, as speaking to his father, "I am no longer worthy to be called your son." What I love about this parable is that before the younger son can say, "make me as a hired man," the father asked the hired men to get the robe, ring, and sandals to cover and celebrate his son.

God is a loving Father just like this. When we find ourselves unworthy to be called a child of God He doesn't leave us exposed. He doesn't leave us looking like our mess. He restores our dignity and celebrates that we are back in His arms. He covers us! Hallelujah!

> But You, O Lord, are a shield about me, My glory, and the One who lifts my head.
> —Psalm 3:3 NASB

The mere fact that the Father runs to his son shows how God has not turned His back to us no matter how dirty or dead we think we are! Daddy is always there waiting and wanting the best for us. Do you believe that? No matter if we have left God, left church or ended up in a mess we never thought we would find ourselves in, Daddy is just waiting for us to come home. Why? Because the Father knows LOVE WILL MAKE US LIVE AGAIN! Though the father thought his son was dead, he had compassion on him when he was found.

Draw near to God and He will draw near to you.
—James 4:8a NASB

O, if the sinner heard this more than just come to my church event. O, if they felt this more than being asked to give in tithes and offering. O, if the church would go to the people in the pigpens of life and clothe them with the same love, grace, forgiveness, and compassion that God did for us, what kind of church would we be? If believers would just go to people like this, what kind of world would we have? If the father was not afraid to embrace his "dirty" son and administer kisses to him, then we cannot be afraid to embrace people like our heavenly Father embraces us.

The text didn't say he showered before he came to his daddy or that he tried to get the money back. He came to him just as he was; smelling like the pigs, smelling like drugs, smelling like sex, smelling like alcohol. But the father said, "My son has come back to life again, he is found."

## PiG PEN iN THE PARK

We were having an outreach for our church in my community and our family decided to go to the nearest park and ride bikes. We took outreach flyers just in case we saw someone to spread the word. There was a middle-aged gentleman sitting on the bench eating, and I approached him and informed him of the outreach. I asked him why he was in the park. He expressed he was an alcoholic and missed his six children and wife. His eyes were yellow from years of alcohol abuse on his liver, so I asked to pray for him. As I prayed, I asked God to heal His son and break this addiction and heal him from any dark places in his past that may have caused him to turn to alcohol. While I was praying this man laid his head on my side, cried, and held me. He kept saying thank you and I told him don't worry about it.

I felt stunned yet, full of purpose that this is what God wants. We must reflect the Father's embrace no matter how bad life may be for others and offer hope.

To be found by the Father wherever we are is the best discovery of our lives.

> "You did not choose Me but I chose you, and appointed you that you would go and bear fruit, and *that* your fruit would remain, so that whatever you ask of the Father in My name He may give to you."
>
> —John 15:16 NASB

On our best day in regards to good works, we still are in the worst state without Jesus choosing us. He chooses us whoever we are, wherever we are.

## DENOMiNATiON DETOX

There was a young lady in our church that came from a highly religious background and was very broken from family and church abuse. I often observed and wondered why she would struggle in worship and discipleship class so much then be free as a bird when it came to fellowship events. I believe it was a challenge to engage in worship and discipleship because worship reveals who you are before a Holy God (Isaiah 6:1-7) and biblical discipleship cuts you with the Word of God to show you where your heart is (Hebrews 4:12). Fellowship is very necessary in the Body of Christ and is often the default mode of Christianity because we meet and eat whenever we can, but fellowship does not tend to deal with the deeper issues of ministry.

At Remnant, we know we are called to minister to the broken in many areas, but mostly those from the heavy religious and spiritually abusive backgrounds. Yet, some people are so "jacked up" from religious manipulation it is more of a challenge to DETOX them from the lies of false doctrine then to share the gospel with an unbeliever. It literally is like a denomination drug they have been addicted to and we have to put them on "DENOMINATION DETOX" THROUGH TRUE BIBLICAL DISCIPLESHIP.

There are many damaging and destructive denominations that *cause dysfunction in people's lives and also cause distortion, preventing people from properly discerning the voice of God.* There is a process of Denomination Detox that we constantly have to walk people through in truth and love. Some reject the "treatment" and return back to toxic churches, false doctrinal beliefs or sinful habits and relationships. For others, it takes months to get free from the mental and spiritual grip in their lives. We deal with many broken people that have come and gone in our ministry that often run from or deny their brokenness such as this case, but we learned *you cannot determine someone else's healing if they do not desire it for themselves.* Broken people must ultimately have to answer this question, "Do you want to be healed?" No matter how long you have been broken our loving Father wants to heal every deep-rooted issue IF you desire to be healed.

> When Jesus saw him lying there and knew that he had already been there a long time, he said to him, "Do you want to be healed?"
>
> —John 5:6 ESV

## iT'S OK TO BE HUMAN

My wife and I talked with this gifted woman and found that because she had been spiritually abused so many times, when we lovingly corrected her she saw me as an abuser. She did not want to deal with her shame and brokenness, so she would bypass us and go through every member of the church who would look past it. We couldn't, because we wanted to help her. I remember telling her, "It's ok to be human." She replied, "No one has ever told me that." No pastor or parent, mentor or church member had ever told her you're human and your going to make mistakes.

Now of course she had direction and correction from her other pastors, but the brokenness was not dealt with in a way where she was restored completely. We discovered this pattern, as she moved from different persons, pastors, and churches. And if she refused our help, it's very possible she refused other's help. However, putting broken people in positions in the church can be very damaging to them and the church. Some people need to sit down at the feet of Jesus and learn their identity in Him before serving in a ministry. This woman was full of abuse and was on the platform of her former churches, where she fooled herself into thinking she had to be a "perfect" Christian by masking her pain because she was serving in ministry. She wanted to look like she had it all together when she was truly falling apart. *If you never investigate the cracks in people you will begin to experience cracks in your ministry.*

Jesus is the only Perfect One there is in the universe and the church needs to deal with pain and not attempt to look so perfect and perform this show called "church." Religion is the greatest show in church. Imagine hearing the famous circus music behind this analogy. The people are coming in for worship service and the ringmaster (pastor) tells the performers to put on their makeup and costumes and to "knock 'em dead." And those performers on the platform are spiritually dying. It's time to take the masks off church.

*The church is so quick to put people in position, but not discover where the position of their hearts and souls are.* At Church of The Remnant, where I am humbled to serve as pastor, we would rather have no one "performing" on the platform then to have people who have not truly encountered the gospel and experienced the healing power of Jesus. It takes time to heal, and the gospel can process us through all the pain.

We will make mistakes and sin again after coming to Jesus and serving in ministry, but the Word is clear, we do not have to practice sin (1 John 3) or sin more so that grace may abound (Romans 6:1). And when it comes to brokenness we have to be honest about the pain and ask for healing. Some may never ask for healing, but we as the Body of Christ must have the discernment to see the need and comfort those while other "church folk" are walking by on the other side (Luke 10:25-37). We cannot neglect the person on the side of the road and go on our merry way to the church service like the priest and Levite. We must be the *Good Samaritan* full of compassion to restore those broken by circumstance or sin.

Jesus had compassion on the people because of their brokenness, but more importantly because they did not have shepherds who were fulfilling their role. *Pastors and leaders must fight for the freedom and healing of God's sheep.* Jesus was not preaching in His church, He was preaching in their churches proclaiming the gospel of the Kingdom that brought healing to the harassed and helpless. Jesus knew we can be in ministry all day and never be ministered to. We need more shepherds who have the compassion to minister to people and not just the capacity to put people in ministry.

> And Jesus went throughout all the cities and villages, teaching in their synagogues and proclaiming the gospel of the kingdom and healing every disease and every affliction. When he saw the crowds, he had compassion for them, because they were harassed and helpless, like sheep without a shepherd. Then he said to his disciples, "The harvest is plentiful, but the laborers are few; therefore pray earnestly to the Lord of the harvest to send out laborers into his harvest."
>
> —Matthew 9:35-38

## HOW DiRTY ARE YOU?

We talked about "How dirty were you?" But HOW DIRTY ARE YOU? I am a realist, and people who are not honest about what sin may so easily beset them are usually the one's struggling in that sin. We have to be honest with our "kryptonite." There are just certain things and people we need to avoid and set boundaries from to keep us living holy. Holy meaning living a life devoted to please God and separate from the world.

What sin are you currently dealing with or what sin is dealing with you? Do you have someone you can confess your faults to and hold you accountable (James 5:16)? The truth is, many people are dealing with someone or something now. Whether it is in thoughts or actions, an unbeliever needs to hear we are not perfect, before or after Christ! We are being perfected, which is maturing in our faith (Ephesians 4:14-15; Philippians 3:12-14; James 1:2-4 ESV). People need to be encouraged by us confessing that we need the Holy Spirit to fill us (Ephesians 5:18) to do His will. It is not our flesh that wants to please God, but the Holy Spirit which God deposited in us at salvation for sanctification.

For it is God who is at work in you, both to will and to work for *His* good pleasure.

—Philippians 2:13 NASB

Now the God of peace, who brought up from the dead the great Shepherd of the sheep through the blood of the eternal covenant, *even* Jesus our Lord, equip you in every good thing to do His will, working in us that which is pleasing in His sight, through Jesus Christ, to whom *be* the glory forever and ever. Amen.

—Hebrews 13:20-21 NASB

I don't think we truly believe how effective the blood of Jesus is. We confess to believing in a work accomplished on the Cross over two thousand years ago before we were born, committed one sin or attended any church service. So if the blood of Jesus is what we believe to be the cleansing agent for every sin past, present and future, that means the sin we commit ten years from now is covered. Why? Because the work is complete! "IT IS FINISHED (John 19:30)!" The Greek word is "Tetelestai:" THE DEBT HAS BEEN PAID IN FULL! As a matter fact, before the foundation of the world, the debt was paid. And the accuracy of God's love continues to circle the earth faster than the speed of light because His love existed before light had a speed.

Blessed be the God and Father of our Lord Jesus Christ, who has blessed us with every spiritual blessing in the heavenly places in Christ, just as He chose us in Him before the foundation of the world, that we would be holy and blameless before Him. In love He predestined us to adoption as sons through Jesus Christ to Himself, according to the kind intention of His will,

—Ephesians 1:3-5 NASB

For He was foreknown before the foundation of the world, but has appeared in these last times for the sake of you who through Him are believers in God, who raised Him from the dead and gave Him glory, so that your faith and hope are in God. Since you have in obedience to the truth purified your souls for a sincere love of the brethren, fervently love one another from the heart, for you have been born again not of seed which is perishable but imperishable, that is, through the living and enduring word of God. For, "ALL FLESH IS LIKE GRASS, AND ALL ITS GLORY LIKE THE FLOWER OF GRASS. THE GRASS WITHERS, AND THE FLOWER FALLS OFF, BUT THE WORD OF THE LORD ENDURES FOREVER." And this is the word which was preached to you.

—1 Peter 1:20-25 NASB

The modern American church does not want to deal with sin anymore because it doesn't make people happy to give in the offering. The mega-church-money-method must keep people happy to give. The most common and "major" sin issue I hear talked about in church circles is the sin of not giving in tithes and offering. Modern prosperity preachers make God out to be some kind of pimp that curses you if you don't give Him what you owe Him. God is not the pimp these prosperity preachers are! These hirelings (John 10:13) are not concerned with the wholeness and healing of people, but rather destroying the sheep, making themselves fat and rich by peddling the gospel with their smooth and flattering talk deceiving naïve people, but their destiny is destruction (Jeremiah 23; Romans 16:18; 2 Corinthians 2:17; Philippians 3:19).

So they leave out that there are consequences for other sins, but say God is cursing you for not giving? That is not our Hebraic curse in the context of Malachi as a whole not just chapter 3. The Lord was not given the best offering by the priests, they were breaking covenant with their wives, doing evil in God's sight calling it good and disobeying God. As a result the whole nation was punished. This is why they were robbing God.

God is more concerned with the well being of our souls prospering and being in good health (3 John 1:2). Can we have nice things, be financially stable and wealthy? Yes, but that's not God's biggest concern. The modern American church has overshadowed the bigger picture of the gospel by preaching this false prosperity gospel. READ THE TRUE GOSPEL and turn off most of the current Christian TV programs and see the TRUE encounters with God the Father, Jesus the Son, and The Holy Spirit that transforms lives forever. The transformation was not just their financial status, but was for their spiritual status. The outcasts, the broken, the blind, the deaf, the poor, the diseased and crippled people were never the same after meeting Jesus and He didn't charge them for the encounter.

## GOSPEL SELECTiVE

When it comes to addressing sin in the church we are now focused on the sin of homosexuality. Although it is a major agenda being pushed in America, the TRUE church must stand on truth. The Bible is very clear on the consequences of sexual sin, and homosexuality and sexual sin is the only sin the Bible tells us to run from. Truth is truth!

> Therefore God gave them over in the lusts of their hearts to impurity, so that their bodies would be dishonored among them. For they exchanged the truth of God for a lie, and worshiped and served the creature rather than the Creator, who is blessed forever.

Amen. For this reason God gave them over to degrading passions; for their women exchanged the natural function for that which is unnatural, and in the same way also the men abandoned the natural function of the woman and burned in their desire toward one another, men with men committing indecent acts and receiving in their own persons the due penalty of their error. And just as they did not see fit to acknowledge God any longer, God gave them over to a depraved mind, to do those things which are not proper, being filled with all unrighteousness, wickedness, greed, evil; full of envy, murder, strife, deceit, malice; they are gossips, slanderers, haters of God, insolent, arrogant, boastful, inventors of evil, disobedient to parents, without understanding, untrustworthy, unloving, unmerciful; and although they know the ordinance of God, that those who practice such things are worthy of death, they not only do the same, but also give hearty approval to those who practice them.

—Romans 1:24-32 NASB


Flee sexual immorality. Every sin that a man does is outside the body, but he who commits sexual immorality sins against his own body. Or do you not know that your body is the temple of the Holy Spirit *who is* in you, whom you have from God, and you are not your own? For you were bought at a price; therefore glorify God in your body and in your spirit, which are God's.

—1 Corinthians 6:18-20 NASB


Though this is truth in scripture, we do become *selective* with what sin we feel is bigger than others. And for homosexuals they feel they are still too dirty for God's love and not accepted in church. Some may even feel they were born that way, but many are that way because of sexual abuse. The reality is, most homosexual people still live in the fear of judgment and live in secrecy, which shows the deeper bondage they are in, but they still need to know they are loved and welcome in our churches. They can be restored and transformed by truth and love. While God loves the sinner, but hates the sin, the person in homosexual sin cannot exchange God's truth for a lie. However, we cannot frown upon them and not on other sins in the world and in the church. It is almost as if people want to have homosexuals sit in one section, liars in another, adulterers on the side, gossipers in the choir. I don't know where the envious and jealous people would sit because we can't see their sin. We have got to do better. They are not any of these labels of sin, they are human beings made in the image, in the likeness of God, who struggle with this particular sin. We are not representing Jesus well, and outsiders notice it. Many people I speak with say, why come to church when you all do the same thing we do out here or even worse? At least we respect God's house and don't come.

Jesus echoed the same thing to the religious leaders in Matthew 23:15 (NASB):

> "Woe to you, scribes and Pharisees, hypocrites, because you travel around on sea and land to make one proselyte; and when he becomes one, you make him twice as much a son of hell as yourselves."

I thank God that times have shifted and we see more multi-ethnic ministries today, but there are still sections of our communities where prejudice divides people when it comes to who needs Jesus. Are you prejudiced when it comes to sharing the gospel? Are you SELECTIVE with who you will love despite their lifestyle? Are you GOSPEL SELECTIVE? We don't want people who don't look like us, talk like us, or live by us to be around us. It is sick. Black churches, White churches, Mexican churches, Rich churches, Poor churches, Mega churches, Small churches. *Sunday is still the most segregated day of the week* (Dr. Martin Luther King, Jr.). I have met with many pastors in meetings and conferences all over Arizona and have discovered that some would not know how to deal with the people Jesus dealt with. I can discern that they like for "their ministry" and "their people" to stay in the normative of "their demographic."

While we are GOSPEL SELECTIVE with those we will share the gospel with or invite to our churches, Jesus broke down every dividing wall of classism, racism, fascism, and sexism in His ministry and died and rose for ALL who would believe (Romans 1:16; Galatians 3:28). *Sinners are not afraid of Christ, they are just not attracted to the lack of authentic Christianity.*

> He said also to the man who had invited him, "When you give a dinner or a banquet, do not invite your friends or your brothers or your relatives or rich neighbors, lest they also invite you in return and you be repaid. But when you give a feast, invite the poor, the crippled, the lame, the blind, and you will be blessed, because they cannot repay you. For you will be repaid at the resurrection of the just."
>
> —Luke 14:12-14 ESV

# CHAPTER 3

## iN CHURCH OR iN CHRiST

As I have kept some of my background as a "preacher's kid" a thread throughout this book, I will confess to you that I was in church, but did not know my position in Christ. When I was ten years old I could feel God tugging my heart towards Him. My home church choir sang "No Greater Love," while visiting a guest church one day and the lyrics struck me, "Jesus went to Calvary to save a wretch like you and me. That's love." Sitting in the back of the church I felt like I was the only one there and God was speaking directly to me. Then, my family and I went to see this Easter play, and when they were nailing Jesus to the cross my heart broke after every resounding strike of the hammer from the large auditorium's sound system. They appealed for Salvation during the altar call, but I didn't want to go down and give my life to Christ because I thought my dad would be mad because it was not my home church. So I walked down the aisle on Father's day June 1988 so that my dad would feel special.

I found myself doing many things that were right in the eyes of my dad and pastor and so the church would be pleased, but looking back this was a very empty feeling. I will return to how the gospel truly changed my life later in this book.

Nowadays, I hear much talk about church planting, church marketing, church positions, but I am burdened that I do not hear more about our position in Christ. We can "do church" well and fit in where we are gifted, but do we know who we are in Christ? We must know who we are in Him. Mary knew her position before Christ, then we find her in a position of humility before Him, and then she is confirmed by Christ that she is forgiven unto salvation and found in Him. This is our position in Christ:

> Blessed *be* the God and Father of our Lord Jesus Christ, who has blessed us with every spiritual blessing in the heavenly *places* in Christ, just as He chose us in Him before the foundation of the world, that we would be holy and blameless before Him. In love He predestined us to adoption as sons through Jesus Christ to Himself, according to the kind intention of His will, to the praise of the glory of His grace, which He freely bestowed on us in the Beloved. In Him we have redemption through His blood, the forgiveness

of our trespasses, according to the riches of His grace which He lavished on us. In all wisdom and insight He made known to us the mystery of His will, according to His kind intention which He purposed in Him with a view to an administration suitable to the fullness of the times, *that is*, the summing up of all things in Christ, things in the heavens and things on the earth. In Him also we have obtained an inheritance, having been predestined according to His purpose who works all things after the counsel of His will, to the end that we who were the first to hope in Christ would be to the praise of His glory. In Him, you also, after listening to the message of truth, the gospel of your salvation—having also believed, you were sealed in Him with the Holy Spirit of promise,

—Ephesians 1:3-13 NASB

Jesus knew what He came to do, redeem and reconcile us to God. Only by being positioned in Him are we seen as being right in the eyes of God. We are positioned IN HIM by the Selection of the Father, the Sacrifice of the Son, and the Sealing of the Holy Spirit. WE ARE IN CHRIST BEFORE WE ARE EVER IN CHURCH! The reality is we are the church after conversion (1 Corinthians 6:19-20).

Even though it is sobering to understand our new undeserved place of privilege, some still do not feel worthy to be *in Christ* even after conversion. So they treat church as a checklist to be right in the eyes of God and avoid certain sins to make them feel as if Christianity is all about what you don't do. This is the same religious asceticism that Paul had to address in the Colossian church because of the rise of Gnosticism, which deemed the flesh to be evil and defending the significance of Christ's humanity and deity.

> Therefore as you have received Christ Jesus the Lord, *so* walk in Him, having been firmly rooted *and now* being built up in Him and established in your faith, just as you were instructed, *and* overflowing with gratitude. See to it that no one takes you captive through philosophy and empty deception, according to the tradition of men, according to the elementary principles of the world, rather than according to Christ. For in Him all the fullness of Deity dwells in bodily form, and in Him you have been made complete, and He is the head over all rule and authority; and in Him you were also circumcised with a circumcision made without hands, in the removal of the body of the flesh by the circumcision of Christ; having been buried with Him in baptism, in which you were also raised up with Him through faith in the working of God, who raised Him from the dead. When you were dead in your transgressions and the uncircumcision of your flesh, He made you alive together with Him, having forgiven us all our transgressions, having canceled out the certificate of debt consisting of decrees against us, which was hostile to us; and He has taken it out of the way, having nailed it to the cross.

When He had disarmed the rulers and authorities, He made a public display of them, having triumphed over them through Him. Therefore no one is to act as your judge in regard to food or drink or in respect to a festival or a new moon or a Sabbath day—things which are a *mere* shadow of what is to come; but the substance belongs to Christ. Let no one keep defrauding you of your prize by delighting in self-abasement and the worship of the angels, taking his stand on *visions* he has seen, inflated without cause by his fleshly mind, and not holding fast to the head, from whom the entire body, being supplied and held together by the joints and ligaments, grows with a growth which is from God. If you have died with Christ to the elementary principles of the world, why, as if you were living in the world, do you submit yourself to decrees, such as, "Do not handle, do not taste, do not touch!" (which all *refer to* things destined to perish with use)—in accordance with the commandments and teachings of men? These are matters which have, to be sure, the appearance of wisdom in self-made religion and self-abasement and severe treatment of the body, *but are* of no value against fleshly indulgence.

—Colossians 2:6-23 NASB

## RELiGiOUS FALLACY VS. REDEMPTiVE FREEDOM

Today, we still want to use religious works to make us feel good in our eyes toward God. This is outward religion that does not engage the heart of God. Our obedience to fulfill His will should arise from our love for Him. Many denominations have mixed salvation and sanctification together, which has caused "Eternal Insecurity" as Dr. Fred Chay shared, who is the professor of hermeneutics at Phoenix Seminary. We have some salvific schizophrenic Christians who are terrified that every sin they commit will cost them their salvation. This comes from bad theological teaching. Yes, some still deal with sinful habits that don't seem to go away, while others may have been totally set free. Yes, some may have even been to a deliverance service, anointed and had demons cast out of them, which is a whole other issue on demonic oppression vs. possession. But why do people still feel "dirty" as Christians?

I would suggest that we as believers still share some of the same struggles unbelievers do. How can I clean myself up before God? Some are still wrestling with the reality of the Word of God embodied through Jesus (the Logos), which He said makes us clean. His Word is what makes us clean and keeps us clean.

We are like Peter, struggling to understand if we are clean after being with Jesus for three years:

Then He poured water into the basin, and began to wash the disciples' feet and to wipe them with the towel with which He was girded. So He came to Simon Peter. He said to Him, "Lord, do You wash my feet?" Jesus answered and said to him, "What I do you do not realize now, but you will understand hereafter." Peter said to Him, "Never shall You wash my feet!" Jesus answered him, "If I do not wash you, you have no part with Me." Simon Peter said to Him, "Lord, *then wash* not only my feet, but also my hands and my head." Jesus said to him, "He who has bathed needs only to wash his feet, but is completely clean; and you are clean, but not all *of you* " For He knew the one who was betraying Him; for this reason He said, "Not all of you are clean."

—John 13:5-11 NASB


Jesus knew exactly who was not clean, Judas. Peter was still going to deny Him three times and yet He calls the Disciples clean. And if this wasn't proof enough that the humble serving Savior wasn't just using water to clean them He echoes the same words in John 15:1-4 (NASB),

"I am the true vine, and My Father is the vinedresser. Every branch in Me that does not bear fruit, He takes away; and every *branch* that bears fruit, He prunes it so that it may bear more fruit. You are already clean because of the word which

I have spoken to you. Abide in Me, and I in you. As the branch cannot bear fruit of itself unless it abides in the vine, so neither *can* you unless you abide in Me."

Jesus was washing them from the point of Him saying, "Follow Me" until His ascension and ultimately until their death as His witnesses (Acts 1:8). But He left the Holy Spirit to remind the Disciples and us of the words that we were to abide, or remain in that keep us clean (John 14:26, 15:26). Even in Ephesians 5 Paul speaks of His words being the cleansing agent for His bride,

> So that He might sanctify her, having cleansed her by the washing of water with the word, that He might present to Himself the church in all her glory, having no spot or wrinkle or any such thing; but that she would be holy and blameless.
>
> —Ephesians 5:26-27 NASB

Jesus said to His Disciples "You are already clean." The Law, legalism, and religion tell us how "dirty" we are, Christ tells us how clean we are by grace. And no matter how "dirty" we may think we can get, the old church used to sing, "THE BLOOD WILL NEVER LOSE ITS POWER." YOU CAN'T DIRTY UP ANYTHING JESUS CLEANED

UP BECAUSE HIS WORK IS ALWAYS COMPLETE. WE ARE ALREADY CLEAN BECAUSE WE ARE IN HIM! NO ONE IS TOO DIRTY FOR GOD'S LOVE!

If we still feel "dirty" then we must come back to the Word of God and be reminded of the cleansing power of repentance and redemption! Romans 8:1 (NASB), *"There is now no condemnation for those who are in Christ Jesus."* We cannot sever our relationship once we receive the free gift of salvation, but we may feel dirty because our fellowship is strained because of present sin in our lives. GOD IS NOT CONDEMNING, HE IS ALWAYS CLEANSING.

When we abide in Christ, in His Words and commandments, not out of religious obligation but because we love Him, this keeps our confidence in Christ that we are clean. The confidence only comes through Christ, not the flesh (Philippians 3:3). I will say that this is not an easy thing to grasp for some believers. It is a challenge for some to receive the love of God so graciously.

This is why Jesus had to come with such a counterculture ministry in His time and even today. The broken, oppressed, diseased, poor, and women could barely have a chance to worship God in the temple, but

God sending Himself through Jesus (John 1:14) to walk and talk with us is like the father running towards his son to have compassion on Him. Jesus was sent because religion wasn't working. God even spoke in the Old Testament that He would circumcise their hearts (Deuteronomy 10:16, 30:6; Jeremiah 4:4). Religion piously portrayed physical circumcision of men to display outward signs that a select few were holy or in covenant with God. God never changes (Malachi 3:6; Hebrews 13:8) in the Old and New Testament regarding a heart covenant (Romans 2:29; 1 Corinthians 7:19; Galatians 5:6; Colossians 2:11). See what Paul shares to the Galatian believers about returning to Judaism rituals (religion) to receive righteousness:

To give a human example, brothers: even with a man-made covenant, no one annuls it or adds to it once it has been ratified. Now the promises were made to Abraham and to his offspring. It does not say, "And to offsprings," referring to many, but referring to one, "And to your offspring," who is Christ. This is what I mean: the law, which came 430 years afterward, does not annul a covenant previously ratified by God, so as to make the promise void. For if the inheritance comes by the law, it no longer comes by promise; but God gave it to Abraham by a promise. Why then the law? It was added because of transgressions, until the offspring should come to whom the promise had been made, and it was put in place through angels by an intermediary. Now an intermediary implies more than one, but God is one. Is the law then contrary to the promises of God? Certainly not! For if a law had been given that could give life, then righteousness would indeed be by the law. But the Scripture imprisoned everything under sin, so that the promise by faith in Jesus Christ might be given to those who believe. Now before faith came, we were held captive under the law, imprisoned until the coming faith would be revealed. So then, the law was our guardian until Christ came, in order that we might be justified by faith. But now that faith has come, we are no longer under a guardian, for in Christ Jesus you are all sons of God, through faith. For as many of you as were baptized into Christ have put on Christ. There is neither Jew nor Greek, there is neither slave nor free, there is no male and female, for you are all one in Christ Jesus. And if you are Christ's, then you are Abraham's offspring, heirs according to promise.

—Galatians 3:15-29 ESV


Religion looks at the outward formality; Relationship finds the inward reality (1 Samuel 16:7). If religion could have saved us Jesus wouldn't have had to come, a relationship was so much sweeter.


## JESUS KNEW HIS "TO"

As recorded in Luke 3:21-23, after the significant baptism of Jesus and the Holy Spirit descending upon Him like a dove, we hear the voice of the Father tell Jesus, "You are My beloved Son, in You I am well pleased." Before one miracle, one sermon, one person following Him, Daddy was pleased. We need to grasp this. Just by our faith in Him, the Father is pleased. Daddy is pleased with you child! You may never have heard that from your earthly parents, but God the Father is pleased:

> And without faith it is impossible to please *Him*, for he who comes to God must believe that He is and *that* He is a rewarder of those who seek Him.
>
> —Hebrews 11:6 NASB

Church dogma has made it complicated to see how clear Christ came for us. Following His baptism, in the next chapter of Luke, Jesus was led by the Holy Spirit to the wilderness to be tempted by the devil and passes the test in forty days that Israel failed after forty years in the wilderness. He leaves the wilderness ready to enter ministry in the power of the Holy Spirit and proclaims what He was anointed "to" do from Isaiah 61:1-2. Jesus only read these few verses because the rest of the text will be fulfilled at His second coming:

> Then Jesus returned in the power of the Spirit to Galilee, and news of Him went out through all the surrounding region.

And He taught in their synagogues, being glorified by all. So He came to Nazareth, where He had been brought up. And as His custom was, He went into the synagogue on the Sabbath day, and stood up to read. And He was handed the book of the prophet Isaiah. And when He had opened the book, He found the place where it was written:

*"The Spirit of the LORD* is *upon Me,*
Because He has anointed Me
*To preach the gospel to the* poor;
He has sent Me **to** heal the brokenhearted,
**To** proclaim liberty to the *captives*
And recovery of sight **to** the *blind,*
**To** *set at liberty those who are* oppressed;
**To** *proclaim the acceptable year of the LORD."*

Then He closed the book, and gave *it* back to the attendant and sat down. And the eyes of all who were in the synagogue were fixed on Him. And He began to say to them, "Today this Scripture is fulfilled in your hearing."

—Luke 4:14-21 NASB

**JESUS KNEW HIS "TO."** The Spirit of the Lord was upon Him because He anointed Him. Anointed means "Chrio" in the Greek, meaning He assigned Him to do His "To!" Messiah or "Masiach" means "Anointed One" in Hebrew, or translated Christ in the New Testament.

He is Yeshua Ha-Masiach. So then we have to ask the questions, what and who was Jesus assigned to?

First, Jesus was assigned to **Preach the Gospel, or Good News**. To reflect on the first chapter of my church background, it wasn't the "Baptist celebration close" that He died, was buried, and got up early for. That didn't happen yet. He preached more than a celebration close. He was preaching the good news to those that were living in such bad times without faith, hope, and the love of God.

Secondly, Jesus was assigned to **Heal or Bind Up the Brokenhearted**. I love what Psalm 34:18 (NASB) says, *"The Lord (Yahweh) is near to the brokenhearted and saves the crushed in spirit."*

The Hebrew describes brokenhearted as being broken in pieces. Jesus came for people whose hearts have been shattered by whatever circumstances or shape it's in. I want to encourage you that Jesus came to put every piece of your heart back together and make it whole again. Every person who mismanaged your heart and gave you empty promises, Jesus was assigned to you! There is healing for your heart through the preached gospel of Jesus Christ. We are not Humpty

Dumpty, Jesus came to put our hearts back together again.

Thirdly, He was sent to **Proclaim Release to the Captives**. In other words, He was preaching or announcing liberty to everyone that was bound by religious, political, or demonic power. In 2 Corinthians 2:14 (NASB) Paul says,

> But thanks be to God, who always leads us in triumph in Christ, and manifests through us the sweet aroma of the knowledge of Him in every place.

God has taken our hearts captive now and He is leading us to triumph wherever we go. This is what people must see, this is how we must live, and this is how we must walk. We have a Savior who grabbed us out of our pit of sin and saved us for His Glory. If people saw you bound before, they need to see you free now! They need to see you changed! They need to hear your redemption story!

I believe God takes us out of addiction, abuse, and adversity to often send us back to be like Moses and bring the rest of His chosen people out of bondage. It is not a coincidence or accident that you survived all the hell you have been through. God always protects

His children because He loves us and has called us to His purpose to save a posterity (Genesis 45:7) or a remnant so they may have the same provision to partake in the grace of God through Jesus Christ. Everything you have been through may not feel good, but it's working together for your good (Romans 8:28). And in God's infinite timing, He only sends us back when He knows we are ready like He did with Moses.

We must *preach* and *practice* this same gospel in a holistic approach that people are healed and offered hope beyond their current circumstances.

Fourthly, there was a *process* to the gospel. We as Christians love when new converts confess Jesus, join the church and then we just send them to a new members class or throw them into ministries. But When do we ask what may blind you from this decision you made? Jesus said I came for **Recovery of the Sight to the Blind**. We must walk with people to make sure they see their faith clearly.

> And they came to Bethsaida. And they brought a blind man to Jesus and implored Him to touch him. Taking the blind man by the hand, He brought him out of the village; and after spitting on his eyes and laying His hands on him, He asked

him, "Do you see anything?" And he looked up and said, "I see men, for I see *them* like trees, walking around." Then again He laid His hands on his eyes; and he looked intently and was restored, and *began* to see everything clearly.

—Mark 8:22-25 NASB

Jesus could have walked away from this man, but He took the time and made sure he saw clearly. It will take time for some people to see clearly after coming to Jesus. The approach of Jesus is so gentle to those with ailments. I love that Jesus took the blind man by the hand first and asked do you see anything. We're going to have to take some people *by the hand* before we *lay hands* and call out the problem. *This is the process of the gospel,* walking with someone by the hand from infancy to maturity as they become disciples.

One thing believers need to do more is just lovingly ask people what is keeping them from seeing Christ and life clearly. A simple touch from Jesus already began the miracle process to bring sight to the man and *then* the miracle was complete by Him laying hands in this case. What simple touches can we implement in our lives so that those with cloudy faith can see God in a whole new way through us?

Lastly, Jesus was assigned, sent to **Set Free the Oppressed**. The Greek word for oppressed is "thrauo" for broken in pieces. The *Concise Oxford English Dictionary* definition is "those kept under subjection or hardship." Not only was He sent for the brokenhearted, but for those who are broken completely. And Jesus closes that He came, "to" **Proclaim the Favorable Year of the Lord**. Jesus ushered in a new dispensation from Law to Grace, and all who believe share in this new covenant and dispensation. Jesus stated in this Luke 4 account that He was the sent One to fulfill all prophecy, which spoke of Him. JESUS KNEW HIS "TO" or in other words He knew His assignment. He was clear about His call, and His clarity was the driving force of the entire ministry He did. Do you know your "To?" Do you have the clarity of your call? His "To" is our to, His Call is our call; to preach the gospel, practice the gospel and let the gospel process people to holistic healing.

# CHAPTER 4

## AM i TOO DiRTY FOR GOD?

You'd be surprised that these plaguing questions and thoughts are still in many Christian's mindset. Am I too dirty for God? Am I too broken to fix? I don't deserve anything from God. God must be punishing me. Does God really love me? You don't know what I've done. God must hate me. If Christians are thinking like this, how do you think sinners feel? Let me say this again, NO ONE IS TOO DIRTY FOR THE LOVE OF GOD.

I have been here too. I used to think God was punishing me for some unconfessed sin in my life or I was doing something wrong. We must stop seeing ourselves as God's problem and as His project of intimacy. God is correcting and disciplining those He loves (Hebrews 12:4-11). God doesn't want us just to be in ministry, He wants us! We are His creation, we are His children, chosen by Him and Daddy just wants time with us.

There is a prevailing problem with the modern American church. We are not grasping the spiritual relationship reality that God desires more intimacy with us. This may be a challenge to comprehend for many that a Holy God wants to be THE INTIMATE SOURCE for our existence and yet we are broken and sinful. I believe this problem stems from experiencing the lack of love and the misunderstanding of God's love. We have had a lack of love in our childhood and churches and the problem seems to be getting worse. We must have an intimate and intellectual relationship with the Father to receive and reflect His love.

> A new commandment I give to you, that you love one another, even as I have loved you, that you also love one another. "By this all men will know that you are My disciples, if you have love for one another."
>
> —John 13:34-35 NASB

If we don't see love, we don't show love. If we don't hear love, we don't speak love. If we don't know love, we don't understand love. We must do our best to exemplify His love.

I will not blame all of our Christian problems on the modern American church, but I do believe the American Jesus is not the same as the Biblical Jesus. And because of spiritual illiteracy we have not intellectually investigated

God's Word to know the true Jesus. The world should hate us first of all and I see too many Christians trying to be accepted by the world or adopting world systems into the church. But also, unbelievers should know we are His disciples by the love we have for one another. This is something that we are failing at in the church. As I said before, we are selective in who we love. I'm so glad God doesn't just stop loving us as people do when we do them wrong.

I believe the issue with the lack of love stems from our homes, which is why the modern church is infested with the lack of this transformational power. There has been dysfunction in every home since Adam and Eve ate the fruit. The lineage of Jesus Christ is full of dysfunction, but we have a "perfection perception" of ourselves that we want portrayed to others like we have it all together.

Many of us have not been loved enough by parents or guardians, therefore we don't know how to receive the love of God. It is hard to receive something that is so foreign to your family of origin. I strongly believe that children gain a perception of God through their parental upbringing.

I only perceived my father in a provider sense that if I needed him for money that's what I went to him for. There were very few father and son talks unless it was about money or ministry. My mother spoiled us into thinking we could get whatever we wanted and that was not healthy either, but I perceived God the same way I viewed my dad. He doesn't care about me, I'll just go to him when I'm in trouble. I am not calling him a bad father at all, he did what he knew was best. Providing financial stability was what he knew best as love. No one loved him like he needed to be loved as a child out of wedlock. But I felt like I had to perform or prove myself in order to receive his love approval, and in return felt like God wanted me to do the same thing. So I would do things to impress him like join the church on Father's day in June of 1988.

## HOW HE LOVES

As I have come to a deeper experiential knowledge about my loving Father God, I discovered time after time He is not like us broken human beings. We don't have to be perfect or perform to earn His love. He simply does because He is LOVE. This is why I have compassion on those who have a hard time understanding a God who wants to love us. It doesn't compute in your mind. It's hard to comprehend when you were abused or abandoned. This is the brokenness that we must be healed from to be complete in Christ and confident in our knowledge about Him.

When did God start loving you? God never started loving you, He *always has and always will* because HE IS LOVE and HE exists before and after time. Therefore, HIS LOVE WILL NEVER STOP either. GOD WILL NEVER STOP EXISITNG AND NEITHER WILL HIS LOVE FOR US! Rest in His Love, Trust in His Love, Be Confident in His Love for you.

We must understand that God is not like any of our parents or past relationships that wanted us to be perfect for them to fulfill promises. God is not like that! Jesus lived a perfect sinless life for us so we are able to receive His love. That's the good news! Yes, it doesn't compute or is uncomprehendable because it's *Crazy Love* as Francis Chan wrote. Why would God relentlessly pursue these broken, sinful, dirty human beings? Because He loves us. It's that simple, but the depth is immeasurable. I was hammered by the Presence of the Lord when I first heard Jesus Culture's version of "How He Loves Us."

**"How He Loves"**

*Verse 1*

*He is jealous for me. Loves like a hurricane I am a tree. Bending beneath the weight of His wind and mercy. When all of a sudden I am unaware of these afflictions eclipsed by glory. And I realize just how beautiful you are and how great your affections are for me.*

*Chorus*

*And Oh, How He loves us so. Oh how He loves us. How He loves us so. He loves us. Oh how. He loves us. Oh how. He loves us. Oh how. He loves.*

*Verse 2*

*We are His portion and He is our prize. Drawn to redemption by the grace in His eyes. If grace is an ocean we're all sinking. So heaven meets earth like a sloppy wet kiss. And my heart turns violently inside my chest. I don't have time to maintain these regrets when I think about the way.*

*Chorus*

*He loves us. Oh how. He loves us. Oh how. He loves us. Oh how. He loves.*

Kim Walker exhortation and prayer . . .

His presence, his love is so thick and tangible in this room tonight and there are some of you in here that have not encountered the love of God,

and tonight God wants to encounter you and wants you to feel His love His amazing love, without it these are just songs, these are just words, these are just instruments. Without the love of God, its, it's just like we're just up here just making noise. But the love of

God changes us, and we're never the same. We're never the same after we encounter the love of God. We're never the same after we encounter the love of God. And right now if you haven't encountered the love of God. And you would know because you wouldn't be the same. You would never be the same again! And if you, if you want to encounter the love of God right now. You better just brace yourself, because He's about to just blow in this place. And we're gonna encounter the love of God right now. So God I speak to all the hearts and I ask God that every heart be open right now, every heart be open, every spirit be opened up to You God. To You and love encounter, a love encounter from You tonight. A love encounter from You tonight God!

Yeah He loves us . . .

THERE IS NO BROKENNESS THAT HE CANNOT HEAL. THERE IS NO MISTAKE THAT OUR FATHER WILL NOT FORGIVE. THERE IS NO PAIN THAT IS BIGGER THAN THE LOVE OF GOD IN CHRIST JESUS.

Who shall separate us from the love of Christ? *Shall tribulation, or distress, or persecution, or famine, or nakedness, or peril, or sword?* As it is written: *'For Your sake we are killed all day long; We are accounted as sheep for the slaughter.'* Yet in all these things we are more than conquerors through Him who loved us. For I am persuaded that neither death nor life, nor angels nor principalities nor powers, nor things present nor things to come, nor height nor depth, nor any other created thing, shall be able to separate us from the love of God which is in Christ Jesus our Lord.

—Romans 8:35-37 NASB

You must be honest about every fingerprint the enemy has placed in your life to victimize you and not allow shame and guilt to shackle you. What you don't reveal God can't heal (Celestia Tracy, *Mending the Soul Workbook*). Your honesty about your past will set you free to victoriously worship God in Spirit and in Truth. Face the brokenness and the dark place and declare your healing from all hurt. You are not alone in your abuse or brokenness. Allow God to slowly remove every layer through time. It is a journey of healing. Many others have been where you are and more importantly, God is with you!

He has not left you for dead. He can and will bring you life, and you will have it more abundantly (John 10:10). He came to save you. He came to heal you. He came to deliver you. He came for you to be loved by Him. His Love is so out of this world that He sent it to this world embodied in Jesus. The loving light of Christ has come to penetrate every dark place in your life.

For God so loved the world, that He gave His only begotten Son, that whoever believes in Him shall not perish, but have eternal life. "For God did not send the Son into the world to judge the world, but that the world might be saved through Him. "He who believes in Him is not judged; he who does not believe has been judged already, because he has not believed in the name of the only begotten Son of God. "This is the judgment, that the Light has come into the world, and men loved the darkness rather than the Light, for their deeds were evil.

—John 3:16-19 NASB

Father, in the Name of Jesus I come to You now on behalf of all of Your hurting children. Father, please liberate the captives now Lord God. By Your mercy and grace, by Your love and forgiveness, liberate Your children to live again. Let the light of Christ Jesus penetrate every dark place and every shackle keeping Your children from true freedom. Father, please do it for them now. Let them know You in full experiential knowledge that You are their healer, their deliverer, and their comforter. You are love God. Let them know You in Your Love. Restore their dignity. Restore their dreams. Restore their destiny by Your grace. Forgive them for not forgiving themselves. I pray they release all guilt, regret, bitterness, anger, and shame. Help them to be whole. Let them be released to greener pastures. Give rest to their soul. Holy Spirit lead and guide them in all truth. Lead them from toxic relationships and lead them away from spiritually abusive churches, physical, mental, and emotional abusive relationships. Father, reconstruct their hearts that have been shattered and mend their souls for Your glory alone. I pray that You would break vicious cycles of family sin and bondage in the Name of Jesus. Set them free from all forms of oppression. Let Your truth make them free. Let Your love be in them. Let Your Word be in them. Let them know they are one with You. Let the Word correct them and draw them to confession and repentance. Let every call and plan You have destined them to be perfected until the day of Christ. Let them know there is no lack in You and they are complete in Christ. We love You Daddy! We thank You Daddy! In the Name of Jesus, Amen!

## BURDEN FOR THE BROKEN

I want to share that this is a journey. I have been where you are, my wife has been where you are, which is why Church of The Remnant was birthed. We came from broken homes and churches, which are still very broken today and we made it out. We are still healing because it is a journey, but as I told you before, God protects His children because He has called us to have a BURDEN FOR THE BROKEN to be healed holistically.

We had to detox from destructive denomination poison that kept us shackled from true freedom. Just think, both of our parents were our pastors and spiritual abuse was what kept us bound more than anything else. Imagine being in a Christian home not knowing if your parents truly love you without perfect performance and then going to the family church, not knowing if God really loves you. My wife felt spiritually schizophrenic at times, as if God was toying with her salvation because their denomination believed you could lose your salvation for many things such as listening to secular music, drinking, or cussing.

We grew up knowing how to play good church. We knew how to save face and not talk about our brokenness. We learned good public relations as preacher's kids. It's sad, but true. I remember a time when I preached at a guest church and shared my testimony about my parent's divorce and my dad told me I shouldn't have done so. I am not saying you need to expose the family's secrets, but there should be some honesty in our families that brings healing. Especially in Christian homes. On this journey of truth and wholeness, not all family members will be open to healing. This is also something you have to embrace and move on with Jesus.

I wrote a song about Christians wearing masks on my album *Follow After Love* called, "Geisha Girls." These are Japanese girls that would paint their faces to dance and entertain their guests. And I feel that we still need to take off our masks and come clean in the church and find our true identity in Christ.

### *"Geisha Girls"*

*Hook*
*Take the mask off church, it's time to come clean*
*No more believers with no purpose and misidentity*
*Gotta know who you are, no more love for the world*
*'Cause they got us dressed up like some Geisha girls*

*Verse 1*
*We can't, cover ourselves like Adam and Eve cause who the Son sets free is free indeed.*
*I'm free from playing dress up, Free from to trying to catch up,*

*Free from these fables of men I'm so fessed up.*
*Everyone yelling change from Obama, but we lost faith in God, like*
*we lost big mama.*
*Sick of the drama like Mary J. Blige and sick of church folk justifying*
*sin lives.*

*Pre-hook*
*We gotta return to our knees and send the prayers up*
*And hope that God hears, then heals and forgives us.*
*Turn the Love of the fathers with the sons, the daughters with the*
*moms, tell the prodigals to come on home.*
*The Word speaks truth to what's wrong from right.*
*Not the letter of the law, but the Spirit giving life.*
*Living life justified, The blood gon' testify.*
*God is not a man that never can lie.*

*Verse 2*
*We can't keep having church when our families are hurt.*
*Then call the carpet cleaners to shampoo our dirt.*
*Year after year we blame the generational curse and wonder why no*
*one believes the power of God works.*
*We Need Forgiveness, Need Love, Need Peace.*
*We need to see the Lord so He can show us the real me*
*No more lost Christians, No more hurt children*
*He came to give life so we can have abundant living*

*Pre-hook*
*Hook*

*Bridge*
*Sunday ain't no masquerade.*
*We gotta be careful of the pain we carry and give it to God and let*
*Him change our story.*
*Sunday ain't no masquerade.*
*We gotta seek out who we are in Christ and stop the charade and*
*let's celebrate life.*

Our loyalty is to God first, not our family. YOU CAN'T FOLLOW JESUS AND FOLLOW FAMILY. Jesus wants us to prioritize our affections towards Him, and family hurt can be one of the biggest distractions from being a fully committed disciple. Jesus uses some harsh language in Luke 14:25-26, but the Greek describes "hate" as loving them less then Jesus:

> Now large crowds were going along with Him; and He turned and said to them, "If anyone comes to Me, and does not hate his own father and mother and wife and children and brothers and sisters, yes, and even his own life, he cannot be My disciple. "Whoever does not carry his own cross and come after Me cannot be My disciple.
>
> —Luke 14:25-27 NASB

## HiS WORDS ARE LiFE

I have shared previously that I was in church but Christ was not in me, or at least I didn't know my position in Him. When I went away to college I was given a new Bible and some devotionals. Then, months after my parent's divorce, I received my call to preach in my second semester. I could hear myself preaching in my bed and said, "God if this is you I will remember everything I heard in the morning." I did, word for word and wrote it out. So I didn't tell anyone and tried to avoid it. I didn't want to be a preacher like my dad, like all the church people said I would always be, and I surely didn't want to make them happy. And who wants to be a preacher their first year in college. So I prolonged the acknowledgment, finished my first year in college and geared up for next year.

In my second year I knew I wasn't supposed to be there. I felt the Lord wanted me in Phoenix to fulfill my call. And then the most gut wrenching emotional year of my life just began to unravel. But as I said before, everything might not feel good, but it's working together for your good. God uses whatever circumstances are necessary to conform us to the image of Christ. Remember that Bible and devotionals I had my first year in school, well

I picked them up and started reading them. Then, I started to come back home almost every weekend for church. And to make it a big spectacle and make my dad proud again, I announced my call to preach on Easter Sunday 1998. Ten years from when I first joined the church on Father's day to be baptized. All this time I was looking for my dad's approval, but really didn't know I had my heavenly Father's.

As I would come back and forth to church on the weekends, I was constantly in my Bible and devotionals. Then, I would come to church service and see inconsistencies with the gospel. We were not doing church God's way. We were not loving each other. We were not seeing people healed. We had a timed program and set structure. I would read and believe about these encounters with God and go to church and see no real transformation. I would read and believe and examine that something was off. I wanted to encounter God's Spirit and power.

I'm thankful for my church history, but I'm more thankful of reading the stories of desperate people who encountered the Son of God and Jesus became part of their history. This is what I believe can still happen today.

It was actually me reading the Bible and believing God at His Word that brought me life because HIS WORDS ARE LIFE. I remember a few years ago when my wife Chrystal was reading the gospels on our couch and she was just weeping. I asked her was she ok. The gospel hit home. She filtered through denomination dogma, religious rules, spiritual abuse and Pharisaical pious leaders, and believed who Jesus really was. Jesus took her hand until she saw men like trees, then laid hands on her eyes and she could see clearly. Jesus said in John 6:63, "It is the Spirit who gives life; the flesh profits nothing; the words that I have spoken to you are spirit and are life." The New Testament professor of Phoenix Seminary Dr. John DelHousaye said, "Ignorance of the Gospels is Ignorance of Jesus." We have to read about Him to form a true theology of Him and let go of the folk theology that is causing no real transformation in our minds.

When we read the Word of God, it cleanses us and also brings us life. Every place where you feel dead or doubtful in your faith, have you read His Words? My wife and I had to filter through *their words, their rules, and their spiritual abuse*, all to discover the Biblical Jesus. Not the American Jesus or the Black Jesus, nor the White

Jesus, not even the Baptist Jesus, or even the C.O.G.I.C. Jesus. THE REAL LOVING JESUS.

Whose words are you holding on to or better yet, whose words are holding on to you? It's time to get free! **HIS WORDS ARE LIFE!** Detox from every false doctrine and ideology that is not of God. SEARCH FOR TRUTH IN HIS WORD AND DISCOVER THAT HIS TRUTH WILL MAKE YOU FREE. This is Jesus' prayer for us:

> "Sanctify them in the truth; Your word is truth."
> —John 17:17 NASB

My wife was liberated from *their words by reading His Words*. These are the Scriptures, which caused her to weep:

> "No one of the rulers or Pharisees has believed in Him, has he?" But this crowd which does not know the Law is accursed.
> —John 7:48-49 NASB

> Therefore some of the Pharisees were saying, "This man is not from God, because He does not keep the Sabbath." But others were saying, "How can a man who is a sinner perform such signs?" And there was a division among them.
> —John 9:16 NASB

## BREAKiNG THE RULES

The Pharisees tried to convince other people that Jesus was not from God because He healed on the Sabbath and they called Him who knew no sin a sinner. Laws! Rules! Traditions! Chrystal realized that her family church would call out everyone's sin and say who wasn't saved, while they were sinning too. What she came to grips with was all the rules, rules, rules they always enforced. She saw the Pharisees all over again. It's what we call legalism. The scales fell off her eyes when she saw Jesus in Scripture for herself, being sinless and treated the same way as she was, forced to "play" by the rules.

Some churches would rather people stay bound and blind so they can continue the spiritual abuse, but when Jesus shows up in your life and sees the need for healing, He breaks all the rules. He breaks the rules of religion because the relationship through grace is so much better. My wife was told that grace was not a part of the gospel of Jesus Christ. And the abuse was so infectious, other family members would tell her she was wrong for believing in grace. Spiritual abuse is just like any other form of abuse, it's toxic, and it's a vicious cycle and hard to break away from. But Jesus is the LIBERATOR OF LEGALISM. Hallelujah!

The Galatian church had this problem too. People were secretly brought in to spy on those who were liberated by the gospel and wanted the Galatians to return to Judaism and works of the flesh.

> But *it was* because of the false brethren secretly brought in, who had sneaked in to spy out our liberty which we have in Christ Jesus, in order to bring us into bondage. But we did not yield in subjection to them for even an hour, so that the truth of the gospel would remain with you.
>
> —Galatians 2:4-5 NASB

> You foolish Galatians, who has bewitched you, before whose eyes Jesus Christ was publicly portrayed *as* crucified? This is the only thing I want to find out from you: did you receive the Spirit by the works of the Law, or by hearing with faith? Are you so foolish? Having begun by the Spirit, are you now being perfected by the flesh?
>
> —Galatians 3:1-3 NASB

I had a questioned posed to me in a meeting with my new friend in the faith named Mark. He asked, "What is more powerful than the Word of God?" Before I answered I know he saw my perplexed face showing you're about to be an associate and not a friend anymore if you say something crazy. Before I could answer he replied for me, "The traditions of men." He was right. Some of us have been so bound by folk theology and lifeless traditions of men that it is hard to see real Biblical power and truth to receive God's love.

> Then the scribes and Pharisees who were from Jerusalem came to Jesus, saying, "Why do Your disciples transgress the tradition of the elders? For they do not wash their hands when they eat bread." He answered and said to them, "Why do you also transgress the commandment of God because of your tradition? For God commanded, saying, *'Honor your father and your mother'*; and, *'He who curses father or mother, let him be put to death.'* But you say, 'Whoever says to his father or mother, 'Whatever profit you might have received from me *is* a gift *to God'*—then he need not honor his father or mother.' Thus you have made the commandment of God of no effect by your tradition. Hypocrites! Well did Isaiah prophesy about you, saying:
>
> *'These people draw near to Me with their mouth,*
> *And honor Me with their lips,*
> *But their heart is far from Me.*
> *Teaching as doctrines the commandments of men.'"*
> —Matthew 15:1-9 NASB

See to it that no one takes you captive through philosophy and empty deception, according to the tradition of men, according to the elementary principles of the world, rather than according to Christ.

—Colossians 2:8 NASB

Chrystal was freed from the traditions of men that kept her bound and from understanding grace. Dr. Fred Chay wrote a short but powerful booklet called *Legalism is Lethal in the Spiritual Life*, which explains how "Legalism is any man-made system, set of rules, mandated expectations, or regulations that promise God will give acceptance and approval in return for, or as a reward for, human effort and obedience." He goes on to say, "that rules without relationship lead to rebellion."

My wife was in the bondage of the LIES OF LEGALISM; she was told that Grace was not a part of the gospel because the real gospel is that you have to follow the rules to be godly. There is so much freedom in grace! Thank God for the RULE BREAKER and LEGALISM LIBERATOR named Jesus. Thank God for Jesus BREAKING THE RULES so we could be healed. Seeing the Pharisees for who they were in Scripture, the Pharisees in her life, contrasted to the sincerity of Jesus is what has set my wife on a journey of freedom in the grace of God. She no longer has to feel like she fails God and has to be perfect to "earn" salvation.

Jesus died for us just as we were, broken, imperfect, dirty, jacked up; the right people He was assigned to heal, free, and release from legalism. God truly loves us for who we are now, no matter how dirty we were or are. JESUS' RIGHT IS ALWAYS THE RELIGIOUS' WRONG. The Grace of God makes no human sense when you are trying to earn salvation, but God did not send Jesus in this world to *make sense*. But by faith it would cause humans to *sense* the graciousness, kindness, mercy, and love of God through Jesus Christ.

## LOVE FULFiLLS THE LAW

Jesus would preach, teach, and reach the "lost" and attempt to share truth with those who supposedly upheld the Law, but His illocution was different when speaking to each crowd and the responses carried reception or rejection. The majority of the "lost" received Him and the majority of those who "kept" the Law rejected Him. We as Kingdom believers are called to have a voice of influence to the church and the unchurched, but those who claimed to know God according to the Law in Jesus' ministry were truly the "lost" and those who had not known the Law were FOUND IN HIS LOVE where the Law and the Prophets hang. "WHO REALLY IS THE LOST?"

The Son of God fulfilled ALL the righteous requirements of the Law that we in our religious human efforts could never fulfill. There were 613 Commandments (The Mitzvot) of ethical and ritual requirements to Remember Yahweh, Reverence His Commandments, and Remain Holy. In Christianity, we have more commonly known and embraced the 10 Commandments and are discovering the depth of richness in the Hebrew Scriptures regarding the totality of Yahweh's commands. Some say the 10 Commandments can be viewed as a brief summary of the Mitzvot. And to be quite honest we can barely fulfill the 10 Commandments let alone 613, but thank God for Jesus who said the Law and the Prophets depend upon 2 great and foremost Commandments, Loving God and Loving People (Matthew 22:34-40). When we truly learn the Law of Love we will reflect the character of God to others and fulfill the Commandments.

Here is some "kingdom math" God revealed to me a few years ago about the Commandments. There are 613 Commandments summed up in 10, 6+1+3=10. Jesus said if we Love God with all of our heart, soul, and strength (Deuteronomy 6:5) and Love our neighbor as ourselves hang the whole Law and the Prophets on these. The equation then takes the subtraction method as 6-1-3=2, meaning LOVE FULFILLS THE LAW. Love God, Love Others.

We should adore and appreciate the life of Jesus more deeply once we understand the Torah and what Yahweh required for His people to obtain holiness. "The Way" (John 14:6) Jesus set the pattern for believers to walk according to the Father's ways and Commandments is seen in the Hebrew word "Halak." Meaning to walk and live a pattern of life following the precepts of God. Jesus walked to show us how God wanted us to live or halak in our daily lives. Once Jesus set the pattern through a perfect sinless life animals were no longer sufficient for our atonement. In this great mystery of mercy, He died once and for all who will believe (Reference Hebrews chapters 7-10). He fulfilled all the righteous requirements and His blood is efficient to wash us clean from our past, present and future sins. Yet, it was the perfect life that Jesus lived that made Him the sufficient sacrifice for our atonement to satisfy God's wrath and judgment for sin.

Jesus crossed every "t" on Calvary's Cross and dotted every "i" with His blood and no one could ever take credit for saving themselves through religious good works or obtain righteousness through the Law (Galatians 2:21, 3:11; Philippians 3:9). Galatians 3:24 "Therefore the Law has become our tutor to lead us to Christ, so that we may be justified by faith." This is why we have to unlearn legalism and learn the grace of Jesus and practice the pattern of the Law of Love:

> "Come to Me, all who are weary and heavy-laden, and I will give you rest. Take My yoke upon you and learn from Me, for I am gentle and humble in heart, and you will find rest for your souls. For My yoke is easy and My burden is light."
> —Matthew 11:28-30 NASB

# CHAPTER 5

## WE'VE LEFT SOMETHiNG OUT OF THE GOSPEL

Through the Scriptures, we established what the gospel was and in the Baptist celebration context, but there is something that Jesus specifically said in the account of the gospels that I do not hear taught or preached. THERE IS SOMETHING WE HAVE LEFT OUT OF THE GOSPEL! This is not heresy, apostasy, or even allegory. *This is a point of practical prescriptive principles to help our perspective of this book.* In my humble estimation, I believe Jesus was more than one-dimensional in what He did and said. He is multi-dimensional. It would honestly take us a lifetime of discovery to search the Scriptures and truths that Jesus revealed and is still revealing through the Holy Spirit. The story of Mary of Bethany, who anointed Jesus' head and feet for burial is multi-dimensional and this is where I want to shift our focus in *Dirty Christianity*.

Mary plays a very significant role in the preparation of Jesus' burial. Whether she knew this was her purpose or not, she was in the right place at the right time for that purpose. Her heart was symbolized in that alabaster box, her worship was poured out like the fragrant oil, and every tear that dropped from her eyes was full of thanksgiving. This is the moment of worship I want to focus on. I am not writing to theologically debate all the details of each account because we miss the simplicity of what I have seen, which will cause the gospel to be more relevant to people who feel unworthy of the love of God. I want you to see her redemption story and then find yours at the feet of Jesus. *There is always a story behind every act of worship.*

Jesus said everywhere the gospel is preached in the world what Mary did would be told:

> "Truly I say to you, wherever this gospel is preached in the whole world, what this woman has done will also be spoken of in memory of her."
>
> —Matthew 26:13 NASB

> "Truly I say to you, wherever the gospel is preached in the whole world, what this woman has done will also be spoken of in memory of her."
>
> —Mark 14:9 NASB

This act of worship happened right before Judas leaves to betray Jesus in the Matthew, Mark, and John accounts. John places the event six days before the Passover. However, Luke has a different chronological placing. I want to focus on Luke's account of the same story. Some will debate and say it is a different account and others will say it was placed here to avoid repeating the event. There are specific reasons I want to draw attention on the account in Luke because of the details of Jesus, Simon the leper, who was a Pharisee and Mary, who has no name in this account.

Who was this woman? The other gospel accounts say her name is Mary, not Mary Magdalene. Mary was a very common name so we call her Mary of Bethany. This event takes place when Simon invited Jesus over for dinner in Bethany before the betrayal of Jesus by Judas Iscariot. Some commentators say Simon could have been setting Jesus up to test Him. In Luke 7:34 Jesus is called a *"gluttonous man, a drunkard, a friend of sinners."* No matter what they may have said about Jesus the sinners never stayed the same, which is why I love this account of Mary. Luke gives the most detailed account of who she was based on her reputation:

The Son of Man has come eating and drinking, and you say, "Behold, a gluttonous man and a drunkard, a friend of tax collectors and sinners!" Yet wisdom is vindicated by all her children. Now one of the Pharisees was requesting Him to dine with him, and He entered the Pharisee's house and reclined *at the table*. And there was a woman in the city who was a sinner; and when she learned that He was reclining *at the table* in the Pharisee's house, she brought an alabaster vial of perfume, and standing behind *Him* at His feet, weeping, she began to wet His feet with her tears, and kept wiping them with the hair of her head, and kissing His feet and anointing them with the perfume."

—Luke 7:34-38 NASB

We have to pause and ask some questions. Why was Mary in the house? What gave her the audacity to anoint Jesus in front of everyone? There was a custom in the Ancient Near East culture where strangers and beggars were allowed to come into your house and eat. She learns that Jesus is near and must go see Him and she has the liberty to do so because of this custom. I don't think it is ironic that Simon is called the leper in the other accounts, and this woman returns to Jesus to show her gratitude for Jesus as Luke also describes in Luke 17:12-19. Only one leper turns back to Jesus to say thank you for being healed.

## WHAT iS YOUR NAME?

This woman is not known by name in Luke's account, but she is known as a sinner, most likely a prostitute. The Pharisees knew her to be a sinner. The anointing of Mary differentiates in Matthew and Mark's account as she anointed Jesus' head and in John's account it shows the similarity to Luke as she anointed His feet. These three accounts denoted the indignation of the disciples because of how expensive the perfume was because they wanted to use this money for the poor:

> Now when Jesus was in Bethany, at the home of Simon the leper, a woman came to Him with an alabaster vial of very costly perfume, and she poured it on His head as He reclined *at the table.* But the disciples were indignant when they saw *this,* and said, "Why this waste? For this *perfume* might have been sold for a high price and *the money* given to the poor." But Jesus, aware of this, said to them, "Why do you bother the woman? For she has done a good deed to Me. "For you always have the poor with you; but you do not always have Me."
>
> —Matthew 26:6-11 NASB

> While He was in Bethany at the home of Simon the leper, and reclining *at the table,* there came a woman with an alabaster vial of very costly perfume of pure nard; *and* she broke the vial and poured it over His head. But some were indignantly *remarking* to one another, "Why has this perfume

been wasted? For this perfume might have been sold for over three hundred denarii, and *the money* given to the poor." And they were scolding her. But Jesus said, "Let her alone; why do you bother her? She has done a good deed to Me. "For you always have the poor with you, and whenever you wish you can do good to them; but you do not always have Me."

—Mark 14:3-7 NASB

Mary then took a pound of very costly perfume of pure nard, and anointed the feet of Jesus and wiped His feet with her hair; and the house was filled with the fragrance of the perfume. But Judas Iscariot, one of His disciples, who was intending to betray Him, said, "Why was this perfume not sold for three hundred denarii and given to poor *people?*" Now he said this, not because he was concerned about the poor, but because he was a thief, and as he had the money box, he used to pilfer what was put into it. Therefore Jesus said, "Let her alone, so that she may keep it for the day of My burial. For you always have the poor with you, but you do not always have Me."

—John 12:3-8 NASB

In these three accounts Jesus says, "Leave her alone because she did a good deed," and "You will always have the poor among you." Judas was stealing and wasn't concerned about the money for ministry anyway. Jesus said the poor will always be among you, but I won't. Jesus is not one-dimensional, but multi-dimensional. He said one thing, but I heard another in these passages. *This is not the time for the needy financially; I have come for those who are in debt spiritually. I have come for a bigger debt that money can't buy. I came to wipe all sin debts away with My blood and bring forgiveness unto salvation. Let this woman prepare Me for My bigger purpose!* Jesus was bigger than an outreach event He was focused on the in-reach of our hearts eternally. *So disciples, leave her alone, this wasn't wasteful this was worship!* They missed it!

Everyone knew this woman by reputation. WHAT IS YOUR NAME? This woman has no name, but she has a label. She's "dirty" in their eyes. What do people know you by? What do you call people? Do you just see yourself by what you have done? Do you see others by what they have done? It is time to get a Redeemed Reputation! Jesus came to change our names. How many times has the Bible not given us names of people who had an encounter with Jesus, but their reputation changed? People may not know our names, but they do need to see our Redeemed Reputation. And we need to stop calling people and ourselves by the labels of sin, mistakes, and failures.

Jesus asks a man full of thousands of demons "What is your name?" in Mark 5:6-14 (NASB):

Seeing Jesus from a distance, he ran up and bowed down before Him; and shouting with a loud voice, he said, "What business do we have with each other, Jesus, Son of the Most High God? I implore You by God, do not torment me!" For He had been saying to him, "Come out of the man, you unclean spirit!" And He was asking him, "What is your name?" And he said to Him, "My name is Legion; for we are many." And he began to implore Him earnestly not to send them out of the country. Now there was a large herd of swine feeding nearby on the mountain. The demons implored Him, saying, "Send us into the swine so that we may enter them." Jesus gave them permission. And coming out, the unclean spirits entered the swine; and the herd rushed down the steep bank into the sea, about two thousand of them; and they were drowned in the sea. Their herdsmen ran away and reported it in the city and in the country. And the people came to see what it was that had happened.

Jesus didn't use the "name" legion to command the demons to come out because that wasn't that man's name. Legion was the label of his situation. But when he was set free the people noticed that the reputation of the man was redeemed as Mark 5:15-20 (NASB) continues:

They came to Jesus and observed the man who had been demon-possessed sitting down, clothed and in his right mind, the very man who had had the "legion"; and they became frightened. Those who had seen it described to them how it had happened to the demon-possessed man, and *all* about the swine. And they began to implore Him to leave their region. As He was getting into the boat, the man who had been demon-possessed was imploring Him that he might accompany Him. And He did not let him, but He said to him, "Go home to your people and report to them what great things the Lord has done for you, and *how* He had mercy on you." And he went away and began to proclaim in Decapolis what great things Jesus had done for him; and everyone was amazed.

We may not know the man's name, but we know WHO changed his name. Once your name has been changed, you don't care who knows your name, but you want everyone to know the Name of Jesus! Unbelievers need to know we encountered the "I AM WHO I AM" (Exodus 3:14) and that's why *I am* changed. I am no longer bound because I AM set me free. I am filled and no longer hungry with fleshy desires because I AM is my Bread of Life (John 6:35). I am refreshed and no longer thirsty for the world because I AM is my Living Water (John 4:10-14). I am walking with Him and no longer wandering in the world because I AM is my good Shepherd (John 10:11,14). I am no longer lost, living in lies, and death because I AM IS THE WAY, THE TRUTH, AND THE LIFE (John 14:6)! Religion didn't change me, but the power of the living God and the sweet presence of the Holy Spirit did. The Father can still *Redeem your Reputation*.

Ask the woman who left her waterpot at the well, because Jesus quenched her ultimate thirst. He was THE SOURCE of her need and her relationships were resources that really never quenched her thirst. *When Jesus meets our deepest spiritual needs we realize we could never be truly satisfied with just our physical needs being met.* She became a convert from a conversation of truth pointing people to Christ after her encounter:

> At this point His disciples came, and they were amazed that He had been speaking with a woman, yet no one said, "What do You seek?" or, "Why do You speak with her?" So the woman left her waterpot, and went into the city and said to the men, "Come, see a man who told me all the things that I *have* done; this is not the Christ, is it?" They went out of the city, and were coming to Him.
>
> —John 4:27-30 NASB

Many Samaritans from that town believed in him **because of the woman's testimony**, "He told me all that I ever did." So when the Samaritans came to him, they asked him to stay with them, and he stayed there two days. And many more believed because of his word. They said to the woman, "It is no longer because of what you said that we believe, for we have heard for ourselves, and we know that this is indeed the Savior of the world."

—John 4:39-42 ESV

It was her testimony that caused the other Samaritans to believe. I could go on and on throughout the Bible. Ask the lepers, ask the lame man, ask the blind man, ask the deaf, ask the crippled, ask the woman with the issue of blood, ask the man with the withered hand, ask the woman with the spirit of infirmity, ask the sinners in Scripture and then *ask yourself. You may be described by something detrimental, but Jesus will change your destiny. You may seemed penned to your problems, but Jesus will give you purpose. You may feel crippled by your circumstance, but Jesus will give you new legs to fulfill your call.* They may not know my name, but He saw my situation and changed it for His glory. *You don't have to prove that you have changed, just live that you are changed!* I remember my uncle asking what I was after receiving Christ as my Lord and Savior, and I gave him my church jargon reply, "A sinner saved by grace." Yes this is true, but he confirmed, "You're a child of God, *that's who you are*." That was music to my heart. Instead of being reminded who I was, he told me who I am. Through Jesus we are changed from sinner to child of God and the Holy Spirit reminds us of this (Romans 8:12-17).

## FORGiVENESS AT THE FEET OF JESUS

This woman, who was known to be a sinner, pressed past every opinion of people and made her way to the feet of Jesus. In the Ancient Near East it was customary to wash the feet of your houseguest since they walked around in sandals in the dirt. This was a job for a slave in their culture and yet we see Jesus as the Serving Savior, washing His Disciples' feet (John 13) right after Mary washes His. Here now is the woman Mary, needing no water, her tears will suffice. I don't know if you have ever been in one of those postures of worship in the Presence of God where the tears are not of sorrow, but flowing because of the grace and goodness of God. Jesus! When you just think sometimes of how good He is, and how much He loves us despite ourselves, that's when *our tear ducts become the conduit to wash His feet.*

As she is standing behind Him her hair is down. For an adult woman to even have her hair down showed signs of promiscuity or disrespect. It also displayed that she was not married because her head would have been covered in this cultural context. However, her humility was exemplified for wiping His feet with her hair. She broke open her expensive alabaster vial and the fragrance filled the room. That's worship! When what we hold valuable can be broken before the feet of Jesus, that's true worship. When all we have worked and saved up for does not compare to how much Jesus is worth for saving us, that's worship in spirit and in truth. When the fragrance of worship fills the room, God is pleased.

The book of Leviticus gives many examples of offerings that would be a sweet smelling aroma to God. Read them and thank God for the dispensation of Law to Grace. We would not have enough time, energy, or livestock to offer up and atone for our sins. God requires one act of worship and that is from our hearts.

Worship is not the music we have in our church services every weekend with screens, smoke and lights, or the best Christian radio stations we listen to during the week. Worship is sacrifice. Worship is not just giving up bad things, but laying good things on the altar as well. Worship was first recorded as Abraham obeyed Yahweh by taking His son Isaac up the mountain to sacrifice him, his promise, and his laughter. Isaac's name means "laughter" in Hebrew (Genesis 22:5). Worship is pouring ourselves out for the glorious grace of our God, and the best worship music is Brokenness. Jesus is the ultimate example of worship:

> Therefore be imitators of God, as beloved children; and walk in love, just as Christ also loved you and gave Himself up for us, an offering and a sacrifice to God as a fragrant aroma.
> —Ephesians 5:1-2 NASB

As long as we are alive, we are a living sacrifice. We are the worship service. Paul shares in Romans 12:1 (NASB):

> Therefore I urge you, brethren, by the mercies of God, to present your bodies a living and holy sacrifice, acceptable to God, *which is* your spiritual service of worship.

This woman is weeping, washing, wiping, kissing, and anointing the body of Jesus and the Pharisee is concerned with Jesus knowing who she was in her sin, her "dirty" reputation. Jesus wasn't concerned about getting dirty with sinners. He was called to them. Simon seemed to know her too well.

> Now when the Pharisee who had invited Him saw this, he said to himself, "If this man were a prophet He would know who and what sort of person this woman is who is touching Him, that she is a sinner."
> —Luke 4:39 NASB

Mary got free from people's opinions! We need this same boldness to press to the feet of Jesus. We have to bypass the distractions of people, the distractions of our past and present, and find peace at the beautiful feet of Jesus. Her kisses showed her deep reverence for Jesus.

> Therefore let us draw near with confidence to the throne of grace, so that we may receive mercy and find grace to help in time of need.
> —Hebrews 4:16 NASB

I have been in church long enough as a pew baby, praise and worship leader, and pastor to know that sometimes it just takes too much for Christians to truly worship God. As if what Jesus did on the Cross is not enough to be grateful. If God doesn't do this or that people are funny with God. God is worthy because we wake up not having to fear death, because we have eternal life in Christ. When I think about the gospel and how much he demonstrated His love towards us, it still brings me to tears (Romans 5:8). We must be grateful to the Most High God that if He never does another thing, He's already done enough. Creation worships God (Psalm 148), but those who have His Spirit need to be pumped and pried to live a life of worship . . . The reality is, God doesn't need our worship but HE deserves it. *Religion Stifles Our Worship; Relationship Stirs Our Worship.*

> **"When God cannot get religious leaders to appreciate Christ, He will use harlots to do so."** —Dr. H. C. Woods

The people who we think don't deserve God's grace and mercy . . . The people who we don't think will "get" church . . . The people who we don't think will be saved . . . These are the people that are grateful for God's love and forgiveness. No one is too dirty for God, but are they too dirty for you? *When we forget what God has done we will fall victim to Pharisaical ways.*

And Jesus answered him, "Simon, I have something to say to you." And he replied, "Say it, Teacher." "A moneylender had two debtors: one owed five hundred denarii, and the other fifty. "When they were unable to repay, he graciously forgave them both. So which of them will love him more?" Simon answered and said, "I suppose the one whom he forgave more." And He said to him, "You have judged correctly." Turning toward the woman, He said to Simon, "Do you see this woman? I entered your house; you gave Me no water for My feet, but she has wet My feet with her tears and wiped them with her hair. "You gave Me no kiss; but she, since the time I came in, has not ceased to kiss My feet. "You did not anoint My head with oil, but she anointed My feet with perfume."

—Luke 7:40-46 NASB

Jesus didn't even turn to the woman until verse 44, but addresses Simon first. The Pharisee was not a reverent hospitable guest and yet he missed the whole story. Remember in the other gospel accounts Simon is known as the leper, meaning Jesus previously healed him. *Simon was focused on her sin and Jesus was focused on her salvation.* I believe Jesus is addressing the church just as He addressed Simon. We must have this focus for the greatest sinner and the smallest sinner. We must love and forgive in the same manner in which we received. WE ALL NEED TO FIND **FORGIVENESS AT THE FEET OF JESUS**.

My wife and I met while auditioning for a church musical. We both won the lead roles, and our characters were in a relationship together. I was a church kid wanting his dad to be home more often rather then doing ministry, and she played a young woman coming back to the church from the influence of gangs. Needless to say we didn't have to search too far to play these roles. It wasn't acting we just had to learn the lines. We were fortunate enough to be a part of another musical years later, which I helped co-write and co-produce called, "The One: The World's First Holy Hip-Hopera." It was the passion week of Jesus to gospel hip-hop and R&B music. One of the local papers did a cover story on us and called it "Jesus Christ Rap Superstar." Through the runs of the musical, over 120 young people gave their life to the Lord and many heard the gospel for the first time through the arts. In the musical, my wife played "Mary" who was a collective version of the women that encountered Jesus in the Bible. I was given the task to write the song for the alabaster box/caught in adultery scene based off of the principles in Luke 4:47.

## "So I Must"

### Chorus

*The One I love, The One I need. I'll pour out all that I have on my knees. This oil I have does not compare to the love you have for me. You forgave me. You didn't shame. You delivered me. You didn't judge me. You showed me love Lord. So I must love more. You forgave again. So I must forgive and receive my healing.*

### Verse 1

*Looking back on the way things were. The pain, the lies, the truth it hurts.*
*How could I do the things I've done I thought were so fun.*
*I wanted to run far from the Holy one. But you caught me and found me and changed me when those demons took control of my peace.*
*Lord I did see by your Holy light, I was healed this night and I thank you.*

### Chorus

### Verse2

*Look at me now a new creature with different features.*
*A smile, joy, love and laughter ever after. How could this be?*
*People used to tell me I was damaged goods and unworthy.*
*But I met someone you said you're worth, My love, My joy, My peace, My touch, My hand, My tears. I'll restore your years the devil took from you because I love you.*

Before the song was ever presented to the director it had us in tears. Both of us had felt like we were damaged goods from our childhood and church backgrounds, but thank God we found FORGIVENESS AT THE FEET OF JESUS.

## YOU DON'T KNOW THE COST

Jesus said in Matthew and Mark, "everywhere in the world where the gospel is preached what this woman has done will be told in memory of her." Mary showed us how not to be so reserved in church. Simon showed us how to be religious with sinners and ourselves. Jesus showed us how much He loves us and forgives us. Point people to the feet of Jesus. TELL YOUR STORY! WE ALL HAVE A STORY TO TELL! At the feet of Jesus shame is set free, guilt is gone, depression is defeated, hurt is healed, and your reputation is restored because of the redemption of Jesus. NO ONE IS TOO DIRTY FOR GOD'S LOVE.

PEOPLE DON'T KNOW THE COST OF WHAT YOU HAVE BEEN THROUGH TO GET TO THE FEET OF JESUS. They don't need to know every single detail of your past, *as long as you know you are forgiven*, tell your story. *Don't you bottle up that worship any longer!* Break open that box and let the sweet smelling fragrance fill your home, your family, your job, your school, your church, and your life. He deserves every tear of thanksgiving. He deserves you lifting your voice in praise. He deserves you reading His Word in meditation. Don't worry what people may think about you, they don't know the cost. *What Jesus did cost Him everything; our worship is a fraction of the cost from the fruit of our lips* (Hebrews 13:15).

His life was poured out before God (Ephesians 5:2) so that He could pour out the Holy Spirit upon all flesh (Joel 2:28; Acts 2). When we pour out He pours in! *We need Passionate Pouring Praise because the Precious blood of Jesus was Poured out as our Propitiation to Purchase us as the Possessions of the Father!*

I believe in the healing power of music, especially pure worship music. I want to encourage you on this journey in the proper perspective where you can have an intimate encounter with God after reading this chapter and experience the Presence of God fill your heart and home. CeCe Winans recorded the *Alabaster Box* and I want to share the lyrics and my experience with you. I strongly encourage you to download the song so it will bless your life as well.

## "The Alabaster Box"

*Verse 1*

*The room grew still as she made her way to Jesus. She stumbles through the tears that made her blind. She felt such pain. Some spoke in anger. Heard for folks whisper there's no place here for her kind. Still on she came through the shame that flushed her face. Until at last she knelt before His feet. And though she spoke no words. Everything she said was heard. As she poured her love for the Master from her box of alabaster.*

*Chorus*

*I've come to pour my praise on Him like oil. From Mary's alabaster box. Don't be angry if I wash His feet my tears and I dry them with my hair. You weren't there. The night He found me You did not feel what I felt when He wrapped His love all around me. You don't know the cost of the oil in my alabaster box.*

*Verse 2*

*I can't forget the way life used to be. I was a prisoner to the sin that had be bound. And I spent my days poured my life without measure into a little treasure box I thought I've found. Until the day when Jesus came to me and healed my soul with the wonder of His touch. So now I'm giving back to Him all the praise He's worthy of. I've been forgiven and that's why I love Him so much.*

*Chorus*

*I've come to pour my praise on Him like oil. From Mary's alabaster box. Don't be angry if I wash His feet my tears and I dry them with my hair. You weren't there! The night Jesus found me You did not feel what I felt when He wrapped His love all around me! You don't know the cost of the oil. Oh! You don't know the cost of my praise. You don't know the cost of the oil in my alabaster box!*

## MY ALABASTER MOMENT

I was in an all night prayer service before I was licensed to preach on December 4, 1999 and remember feeling the Lord's presence in the room so strongly. As I sat on the floor with the other licentiates, my eyes were closed and I heard people weeping and worshipping because God was intimately touching them. I remember simply praying, God what about me? Will you touch me? And then it happened, the sweet presence of my heavenly Daddy touched my soul in a way I could have never imagined. I was fasting that week and anticipating God touching me for this call I was about to dedicate my life to, but never imagining Him filling me with so much joy and His Spirit. So much so I received with the evidence of speaking in tongues. CeCe Winans put it best as she told Mary's story and then one of personal application and experience . . . **YOU WEREN'T THERE, THE NIGHT HE FOUND ME . . . YOU DON'T KNOW THE COST!**

And as I sit here listening to this song again and reflecting on Mary's story of redemption and my own, I am free to worship, not prohibited by religion or reputation to pour out my worship as I weep again on the redemption of the gospel of Jesus Christ that has gripped my heart. WE ARE FORGIVEN AND LOVED BY THE CREATOR OF THE UNIVERSE AND HE WANTS US TO CONTINUE TO REMEMBER HOW MUCH HE LOVES US AND OUR RESPONSE SHOULD BE THIS; THERE IS NOTHING WORTH MORE THAN GIVING YOU ALL OF ME BECAUSE YOU GAVE YOUR ALL TO SAVE ME!!!

Sometimes you need to go back to see where God has brought you from. That's where real worship takes place. *It's not in a church, it's in the depths of your heart and mind where it was just you and JESUS, you and Love, You and Forgiveness, You and Grace, You and Joy, You and Truth, You and Hope, You and Faith, You and Transformation.* God has taken me back to the floor where I found FORGIVENESS AT THE FEET OF JESUS. I encourage you to tell your story to others, but most importantly never forget to forego religious rules and reputation and worship God for all He is worth to you! Break your worship open!

While Simon was making it known that she was a sinner, Jesus *corrects him* and *confirms her* by making it public that the woman who they knew as a sinner was now to be known as forgiven:

> "For this reason I say to you, her sins, which are many, have been forgiven, for she loved much; but he who is forgiven little, loves little." Then He said to her, "Your sins have been forgiven." Those who were reclining *at the table* with Him began to say to themselves, "Who is this *man* who even forgives sins?" And He said to the woman, "Your faith has saved you; go in peace."
>
> —Luke 7:47 NASB

# CHAPTER 6

## COVERED

No matter if your story was public or private, God always covers His children. Sin causes us to run and hide from God and we try our best to cover ourselves, conceal our sin, and barely confess it, but do so through blame shifting. Look at Adam and Eve:

> Then the eyes of both of them were opened, and they knew that they were naked; and they sewed fig leaves together and made themselves loin coverings. They heard the sound of the LORD God walking in the garden in the cool of the day, and the man and his wife hid themselves from the presence of the LORD God among the trees of the garden. Then the LORD God called to the man, and said to him, "Where are you?" He said, "I heard the sound of You in the garden, and I was afraid because I was naked; so I hid myself." And He said, "Who told you that you were naked? Have you eaten from the tree of which I commanded you not to eat?" The man said, "The woman whom You gave *to be* with me, she gave me from the tree, and I ate." Then the LORD God said to the woman, "What is this you have done?" And the woman said, "The serpent deceived me, and I ate."
>
> —Genesis 3:7-13 NASB

Adam and Eve could never sufficiently cover themselves nor conceal their sin from God. We serve a God who pursues us even when we disobey. Why? Because He is a relational God! God knew where Adam was and only wanted him to confess why he was hiding. In Genesis 1:1 God in Hebrew is Elohim, describing Him as a powerful creator. When the Genesis narrative breaks in 2:4 there is a new characteristic added to Elohim, Yahweh. YHWH is known as the Tetragrammaton adding the vowel points from Adonai later to pronounce God's Name in Hebrew. Yahweh is the proper name of God and points to the characteristics that He is a relational covenant keeping God. At the point when mankind was formed out of the dust, the Lord God (Yahweh Elohim) would remain faithful to Adam and Eve knowing they would disobey Him.

*God knows how to keep promises when we will fail to keep ours and it is in His nature to cover us and not leave us exposed.*

> The LORD God made garments of skin for Adam and his wife, and clothed them.
> —Genesis 3:21 NASB

Jesus' name means Yahweh Saves or Yahweh is Salvation, and in Matthew 1:23 He is to be called *Immanuel* meaning, "God with us." So Jesus' name speaks to our relational God being with us to fulfill His promise to protect and save us. This is our covenant keeping relational God! He *comes to us* and *doesn't run from us,* and if we know this about the Father we should run to Him. He knows that fig leaves will never cover the shame of sin, so He must be our covering.

> He will cover you with His pinions, And under His wings you may seek refuge;
> His faithfulness is a shield and bulwark.
> —Psalm 91:4 NASB

## DiRTY CONFESSiON

When I use the word "dirty" I am using it to describe the state, label, or category of how people view certain sinners or how we perceive ourselves. If we start searching through anyone's house, car, or office we will find a little dirt somewhere. In other words, there is "dirt" all over the place and someone needs to be honest about it so we can clean up this mess and share the true power of the gospel. Sometimes I use "dirty" in a good context that makes us relevant to sinners who don't see Christians as perfect little saints, thus, *Dirty Christianity*.

That doesn't mean we become all things to all men to win some by cussing, drinking, and clubbing. This is not a book to expose any denomination or air dirty laundry. This is an honest approach of not being ashamed of relaying the gospel with our redemption stories.

> To the weak I became weak, that I might win the weak; I have become all things to all men, so that I may by all means save some. I do all things for the sake of the gospel, so that I may become a fellow partaker of it.
> —1 Corinthians 9:22-23 NASB

If any of you reading this book have been in a very religious or Pharisaical church, you already know if you fall into sin you will be exposed. It's just the nature of the beast, especially if you are in leadership. My wife and I had our first son out of wedlock and I was the interim youth co-coordinator in my dad's church at the time. Now, I will say this precious woman of God prayed with us before the pregnancy happened a few times and warned us to stop having sex. Well, we would stop, then start again. I even, wrote a song about it based on Romans 7 called, "What's Your Desire?"

> *Hook*
> *When I try to do right, I just seem to do wrong. Jesus can You help me so I can be strong. I need to die to my flesh, this battle's been too long. Victory is mine I wanna sing my song. What's Your Desire?*

My wife (girlfriend at the time) wanted to move out of state to protect my "church image." I refused to let her leave in shame to protect my image and vowed to protect and defend her. *I learned to care less about saving face because we have saving grace.* Because I was in leadership I knew my dad would make me stand before the church and confess our sin. Some of you will agree this is how discipline should be done in the church, but this is not how God covers us. Do we expose gossipers, liars, porn addicts, abusers, etc. before the church? No. Only when someone gets pregnant or the proof of the sin is so evident and the church needs to save face do we bring the "sinner" forward. Some may disagree, but there have been people that have dealt with sexual sin in our church and I lovingly dealt with them in truth behind closed doors to restore them in meekness (Galatians 6:1-5). The Bible does give clear instructions on how to remove someone from the church if things out of hand with immorality, but that is not the context of our story (Ref. 1 Corinthians 5; 2 Corinthians 2:5-11). I know there are consequences for our sin and we as leaders have to be held to a higher degree, but not like this. And it is always in regards to sexual sin that someone is brought before the church. This is the church's sensational spectacular sin. Remember the woman caught in the act of adultery (John 8:1-11)?

The night of our "Dirty Confession" was during a Wednesday night service. We shared it with the youth group, and they forgave us with warm hearts for being honest. Then we had to stand before the adult church service. My dad, who was our pastor, wanted me to have a written statement to review what I was going to say before this day, but I refused the church "P.R. campaign" and wanted to speak from my heart. On one side stood Chrystal's family, and on the other mine, with my dad standing next to me in the middle aisle in front of the altar. I read from Philippians 3:12-14 that night, before I began my dirty confession in the context of leaving my past behind and pressing towards the mark. Some of the things I said was that what we had done in private resulted in pregnancy and I loved this woman and the baby is not a mistake, and we were planning to get married before this happened. We repented to God and believe He has forgiven us and apologized to the young people. I didn't say too much after that, but ended with this, "If you have any comments or questions leave them at the foot of the cross." I hung my head in shame and then some church members stood up and applauded. I know they were not applauding for the pregnancy, but that I could boldly stand in God's grace and confess my sins. Then my dad who was my pastor, and boss at the time, grabbed the microphone from me and sternly said, "I don't see no need for no applause!" And after that I could not hear anything else he said. I hung my head even deeper and began to weep and my mother whisked Chrystal and I away to the prayer room. My dad came back there and was furious for what I said. I guess he wanted me to condemn myself, but I couldn't. The worst thing about this story is that my dad committed adultery and never stood before the church and confessed his sin. So you can imagine the anguish my mother felt for me. This was one of the craziest nights of our lives, but God is still good.

## iT WAS ALL FOR HiS GLORY

I was not fired because it was only a temporary position and was able to finish my term with the other youth coordinators. I did not quit the ministry because of the shame, but my wife and I learned to be attracted to sinners who are not covered by love and grace.

There was even a guy that told me thank you for not giving up on God. When I see you up there leading praise and worship, it gives me hope because he had a baby out of wedlock and was told his life was over. Later on when church ministers would ridicule me, my dad would come to my defense and I appreciated that. I even got hate mail from a church member for continuing in the ministry. I used to sing Donnie McClurkin's song, "We fall down, but we get up" and the letter said, "you should sing, "you fell down and you messed up." We could have hated God and the church because of all this ridicule and shame, but IT WAS ALL FOR HIS GLORY. Our heavenly Father covered us and our first son Josiah with a canopy of grace.

We eventually left my dad's church and started the journey of healing at my wife's church where we met auditioning for the play. This is the place where she found refuge after leaving her father's church where she experienced spiritual abuse. It was all for His glory that we met there and found greener pastures at The River of Life. The healing process began as we were received with open arms of restoration in that season. We would later return to my home church where I became the full-time minister of children, youth, and young adults.

What I discovered in standing before the church is I got "dirty" and felt free to not live in a little Perfection Perception! I felt my religious mask finally coming off. Even the core young people from that time have joined Church of The Remnant and are growing in the grace of God. I asked them why they didn't return to my dad's church where they grew up as well, and they said because he never confessed his sin like he made you. That blew me away.

God works all things together for our good. He was using that moment to conform us both more to the image of Christ. I don't have regret or bitterness about it, we learned from it. Secret sin will be exposed, but you can still be covered. No, it didn't feel good, but to have another chance for my wife and I to pour into these young adults and help them build godly families is amazing. Through the good, the bad, and the ugly, IT WAS ALL FOR HIS GLORY.

## DiRTY DAViD

David knew how to repent to God and God alone. He was a man after God's own heart because his heart was broken for the things of God. Since the Holy Spirit was not available to everyone in the Old Testament, David knew through Saul's sin that His Spirit could be taken away, he pleaded to keep it. His sacrifice was his broken and contrite heart. This offering is one God never rejects. This is the worship music in God's "IAMpod."

Psalm 51 (NKJV)

Have mercy upon me, O God,
According to Your lovingkindness;
According to the multitude of Your tender mercies,
Blot out my transgressions.
Wash me thoroughly from my iniquity,
And cleanse me from my sin.

For I acknowledge my transgressions,
And my sin *is* always before me.
Against You, You only, have I sinned,
And done *this* evil in Your sight—
That You may be found just when You speak,
*And* blameless when You judge.

Behold, I was brought forth in iniquity,
And in sin my mother conceived me.
Behold, You desire truth in the inward parts,
And in the hidden *part* You will make me to know wisdom.

Purge me with hyssop, and I shall be clean;
Wash me, and I shall be whiter than snow.
Make me hear joy and gladness,
*That* the bones You have broken may rejoice.
Hide Your face from my sins,
And blot out all my iniquities.

Create in me a clean heart, O God,
And renew a steadfast spirit within me.
Do not cast me away from Your presence,
And do not take Your Holy Spirit from me.

Restore to me the joy of Your salvation,
And uphold me *by Your* generous Spirit.
*Then* I will teach transgressors Your ways,
And sinners shall be converted to You.

Deliver me from the guilt of bloodshed, O God,
The God of my salvation,
*And* my tongue shall sing aloud of Your righteousness.
O Lord, open my lips,
And my mouth shall show forth Your praise.
For You do not desire sacrifice, or else I would give *it;*
You do not delight in burnt offering.
The sacrifices of God *are* a broken spirit,
A broken and a contrite heart—
These, O God, You will not despise.

David adored the mercy and lovingkindness of God, then acknowledged his sin. The goodness of God leads men to repentance (Romans 2:4). I don't know if he confessed before a Wednesday night service, but people did know King David's public sin. *We must thank God for the Nathan's in our lives* (2 Samuel 12)! This precious woman of God who warned us about our sexual waywardness was just doing what God prophetically called her to do. She was a Nathan. To make the story sweeter, her daughters are the ones who were in the youth group and are now a part of our church. I told you it was all for His glory because He works everything together for our good.

## ON PURPOSE FOR PURPOSE

Even if we are wounded and exposed, don't quit on God and what He has called you to. You don't know who needs you to survive so they can live. That's Remnant; the survivors to help others live again! Ask Joseph if the pit felt good. Ask him if the prison felt good. Ask him if family plotting to kill him felt good, but he didn't give up on his dreams.

*You can't kill God's dreamers!* No matter what family, friends, or foes plot against you, You can't kill God's dreamers! Everything is for a purpose. Whether you caused it or God designed it, everything we go through serves a purpose. We may not see it now, but faith will bring it into focus. If God calls you, He calls you ON PURPOSE FOR PURPOSE. If Joseph wasn't betrayed and put into a pit he wouldn't be in the position of power later on. The pit was on purpose, the pain was on purpose, the prison was on purpose, Potipher's wife was on purpose, Pharaoh's house was ON PURPOSE FOR PURPOSE.

When we are called by God there is a great sense of joy in the initial acceptance or at the dreams He may give us. However, there are many unexpected challenges that come with the call and God does not reveal many of them to us. Don't be afraid to answer the call because of the unforeseen challenges. We must simply hold on to what we initially saw and heard and follow by faith on the journey. Everything we go through is ON PURPOSE FOR PURPOSE! We may not have known all of what our call would contain, but Jesus did! Joseph just had a dream and didn't know he would be betrayed by his brothers, but later he knew what they meant for evil was for God's good (Genesis 50:20). I may not have known the extent of my call initially, but through the progressive revelation of keeping the faith and enduring through persecution, joy is being perfected (James 1:2-4). *Progressive Revelation gives you a Prophetic Perspective.* When you can look back and say it was for my good because I'm still here for a purpose *That's a Prophetic Perspective*!

Joseph didn't know and I didn't know, but Jesus knew what they would go through. He knew that when Joseph dreamed the dream he wouldn't give up. Jesus knew that when I heard the call I would keep hearing His voice to hold on for what He has showed me. Why? Because He calls us ON PURPOSE FOR

PURPOSE TO BE LIKE HIM. And we know that ALL things work . . . Together . . . For the good . . . of Them that LOVE GOD . . . and who are THE CALLED . . . ON PURPOSE FOR PURPOSE . . . FOR HIS PURPOSE (Romans 8:28)! FORGIVE, HEAL, AND LET IT GO! Hold on to every dream that God has placed inside of you. People are counting on you to not give up hope on your dreams.

> God sent me before you to preserve for you a remnant in the earth, and to keep you alive by a great deliverance.
> —Genesis 45:7 NASB

> But Joseph said to them, "Do not be afraid, for am I in God's place? As for you, you meant evil against me, *but* God meant it for good in order to bring about this present result, to preserve many people alive. So therefore, do not be afraid; I will provide for you and your little ones." So he comforted them and spoke kindly to them.
> —Genesis 50:19-21 NASB

David knew his destiny wasn't over because of his iniquity, but he didn't want his fellowship with God to be strained by his sin. David prayed that the joy of salvation would be restored. This is what some of you need to pray. You've been so hurt or may have gone so far back into some sin that you don't even get excited about the Lord anymore. Pray that the Lord would restore your joy! Jesus was called to us ON PURPOSE FOR OUR PURPOSE to have Joy in Him. He was crucified because of the JOY that was set before Him He endured the cross (Hebrews 12:1-2). He knew His CALL CALLED for Pain and Persecution, but He also knew His call included PROMOTION. Sin brought David down, but He asks God to restore him. Sin brought Jesus down, but the Holy Spirit restored and resurrected Him. Sin or the lack of joy in our Salvation should never keep us down for too long. Give it three days and then declare your "Early Sunday Morning!" Your resurrection needs to happen through repentance just like David.

"Dirty David" shows us what our response of restoration through repentance should be towards sinners. Verse 13, *"Then I will teach transgressors Your ways, and sinners will be converted to You."* In today's context David could say, "I was "dirty" for so many reasons, but I repented and I am restored." People need to see your joy again. Don't let sin or shame steal it. Repent and stand in the confidence of the grace of God that He has forgiven you and that He will keep you from falling.

If we say that we have no sin, we are deceiving ourselves and the truth is not in us. If we confess our sins, He is faithful and righteous to forgive us our sins and to cleanse us from all unrighteousness. If we say that we have not sinned, we make Him a liar and His word is not in us.

—1 John 1:8-10 NASB

Now to Him who is able to keep you from stumbling, and to make you stand in the presence of His glory blameless with great joy, to the only God our Savior, through Jesus Christ our Lord, be glory, majesty, dominion and authority, before all time and now and forever. Amen.

—Jude 24-25 NASB

# CHAPTER 7

## DiRTY JESUS

Religious leaders could not stand Jesus and His Disciples. They were mad that He healed on the Sabbath, angry the Disciples didn't wash their hands, furious that He ate with sinners, etc. They were indignant that they were losing their fear-filled manipulative control by His liberating love. They were mad He was breaking their laws by amazing grace, while their temple and synagogue services were not working to heal anyone and there was no real encounter with God that brought transformation. *Jesus didn't need the building to bring transformation.* He was and is the God of the Church. He came to serve the church, not to have a good church service.

What kind of God leaves His people broken in His house? What kind of God leaves His people hurting and oppressed in church? What kind of God looks over spiritual abuse? Not our loving God! There are many people in churches like this around the world and those locally who I counsel, which put all the responsibility on God to inform them to leave these places. If you are in a physical, emotional, or sexual abusive relationship you need to get help and leave. Why is it different in a spiritual abusive relationship? Does God have to tell you to leave? No! God wants to you make a journey to freedom and get free from toxic denomination and pastoral relationships. I understand you want to wait on the "voice of God" to tell you, I've been there too, pray and fast about it, seek counsel, AND MAKE A DECISION while all the signs are saying exit. That is God speaking! But let me share this, dysfunction in the church can distort the voice of God. You may think God wants you to stay, but you may not be hearing Him clearly. It's ok to want spiritual relief. Your loyalty is not to your family's fellowship, traditional ties, or dysfunctional and destructive denominations. *I would strongly argue that not every place, which is called a house of God, is His Holy residence.*

Reading through the gospels we find many sinners attracted to Jesus and religious leaders wanting to attack Him. Jesus was approachable, which is why He attracted the unlikely characters that the church of His time ridiculed. Demoniacs weren't afraid to approach Him, the centurion man, officials, the lepers, fathers, mothers; friends were bringing people to Jesus. Religious leaders hated this. But remember Jesus knew His "to" and when you know what you are called to do, *everything and everyone to fulfill your purpose is attracted to you.* Jesus didn't need to have a church building to take up an offering either. People were transformed and they gave to His ministry out of appreciation and not obligation (Luke 8:1-3). Jesus knew how to seek out His "dirty" demographic:

> As Jesus went on from there, He saw a man called Matthew, sitting in the tax collector's booth; and He said to him, "Follow Me!" And he got up and followed Him. Then it happened that as Jesus was reclining *at the table* in the house, behold, many tax collectors and sinners came and were dining with Jesus and His disciples. When the Pharisees saw *this,* they said to His disciples, "Why is your Teacher eating with the tax collectors and sinners?" But when Jesus heard *this*, He said, "*It is* not those who are healthy who need a physician, but those who are sick. "But go and learn what this means: 'I DESIRE COMPASSION, AND NOT SACRIFICE,' for I did not come to call the righteous, but sinners."
>
> —Matthew 9:9-13 NASB

Sinners know who is truly authentic! Hang out with sinners for a while, and they will let you know if you're an authentic Christian. Jesus was approachable, and if we as Christians do not attract sinners to us then we must lack some qualities that Jesus had. Love is Attractive. Hope is Attractive. Authenticity is Attractive.

## ATTRACTED TO AUTHENTiCiTY

My mother and I were leaving my house one night after she took care of our children. While walking through the front yard, these young people were quickly approaching behind us. I said, "Come on mom we gotta go, we gotta move." Yes I was scared because there were a few big dudes. Ha ha! After dropping her off and returning home I was listening to some worship song about how good God was and the young people were in the parking lot by my space. As I went in the back way to our house I heard the Lord ask, "You can listen to how good I am, but can't tell them about Me?" I immediately told my wife, "I'm going to witness to these young people outside. Pray for me."

I greeted the biggest one, who was walking behind us when my mom left and asked what they had going on that night. He seemed to be the leader. One of their friends just got out of jail and they were going to celebrate. There was a young lady who was apparently drinking was trying to hit on me, another young man was blowing smoke in my face and more friends began to migrate there. While I was talking to the young man a condom fell out of his pocket. I asked what he was doing with that (like I didn't know). He said, "About to get up in something." I then asked if he knew that fornication was a sin. He said, "No, what's that?" So I explained. Then I asked if he was saved and he said he had been baptized years ago in another church. I questioned, "And you did not know this was sin?" He humbly said, "No." Then the party crew was getting anxious so I asked to pray for them before they left. He then shouted to the sixteen other young people, "Ay, y'all come over here my pastor is about to pray!" I said, "So I'm your pastor now?" He said, "Yeah, because you're the first person who told me the truth." I was truly humbled and honored by this. As the large group of teenagers gathered in a circle to pray, they respectfully removed their hats and bowed their heads. I felt so full of purpose as we prayed together. I never knew if I would see them again, but I prayed that the Holy Spirit would send people to water those seeds that were planted.

This young man came back to the neighborhood about a year later and wouldn't you know he moved next door to me. I was learning what I am sharing with you; people respect authenticity. I wasn't trying to condemn him, just point him to the truth. People are ATTRACTED TO AUTHENTICITY. He recently came to our church and said that he felt that I was preaching directly to him. The Holy Spirit was, I served as the conduit to lead him to truth. If I condemned him or his friends for the sex, smoking, and drinking he may have never come to our church. *The reality is he came to church because the authentic church came to him.* Jesus approached people with authenticity. Even if they were wrong, He did it in truth and love. They can come as they are, but when you encounter Jesus you never stay as you are.

> Rather, speaking the truth in love, we are to grow up in every way into him who is the head, into Christ,
> —Ephesians 4:15 ESV

## JESUS DiDN'T COME TO SEEK SAiNTS, SAiNTS SHOULD BE SEEKiNG HiM!

Jesus was constantly questioning the Disciple's faith in Him. Sinners didn't seem to have this issue. When you see authenticity in action it is attractive. Like Jesus, as pastors we spend so much time managing believer's issues and teaching them to continue to believe in God that it's often a challenge to reach sinners outside of the church. Thank God for Jesus' model that you have to teach some disciples along the way. It just baffles me how almost every sinner Jesus encountered left changed and He had to repeat Himself over and over to those that were already following Him. Look at the Epistles, they are written to believers. Yes we need to be encouraged, exhorted, and edified, but when will an encounter with a Holy Jesus set our faith ablaze? JESUS DIDN'T COME TO SEEK SAINTS; SAINTS SHOULD BE SEEKING HIM (Matthew 9:12-13)! He came to seek sinners and bring them to repentance.

Sinners got it. He was here for them. You have to get this too. JESUS GOT DIRTY FOR US! He took on ALL sin so that we would never have to feel the wrath of God. He became sin who knew no sin (1 Corinthians 5:21), but knew sinners. Our sinless, spotless, innocent Jesus took on our dirt, our guilty stain, our sin, our shame and experienced the rejection we should have felt from the Father for the joy of us being saved. HE BECAME "DIRTY JESUS" SO GOD WOULD ALWAYS SEE US "CLEAN CHILDREN" AS HE SAW HIS SON, Perfect, Precious, Blameless, Blessed; ONLY by receiving Him by faith does God see us like this. Hallelujah!

All the shame we should ever feel for sin or abuse Jesus has dealt with it on the Cross of Calvary once and for all (Romans 6:9-10; Hebrews 7:24-27, 9:11-12, 24-28; 1 Peter 3:18). Tell your shame you have been dealt with! Tell your condemnation you have been dealt with! Tell your fear you have been dealt with on the Cross of Christ. TETELESTAI! IT IS FINISHED! I HAVE VICTORY!

Former sinners who encountered Jesus seemed to have instant track shoes. They ran to tell the gospel immediately. What is hindering you from running to tell your story? Run to Him, Run for Him, Run with Him, then Run for them. Run knowing the victory is already yours.

> Therefore, since we have so great a cloud of witnesses surrounding us, let us also lay aside every encumbrance and the sin which so easily entangles us, and let us run with endurance the race that is set before us, fixing our eyes on Jesus, the author and perfecter of faith, who for the joy set before Him endured the cross, despising the shame, and has sat down at the right hand of the throne of God.
>
> —Hebrews 12:1-2 NASB

Jesus knows what sin feels like, He knows what condemnation feels like, He knows what rejection from the Father feels like so we would NEVER have to feel this from God. So when you share your redemption story there is no shame because Jesus took it for you. YOU ARE NOT DIRTY ANYMORE!

## TEMPLE CLEANSiNG

Jesus was tired of the oppression of the broken, outcast and poor, and the climax of His ministry happened when He cleansed the temple and the chief priests and scribes wanted to kill Him (Mark 11:18). This event occurred when thousands of people would have gathered to offer their sacrifices at the temple, but the Gentiles had a designated section in the outer courts of the temple for their sacrifices. The doves that were being sold were the offering of the poor. The moneychangers were distracting their worship to God. This gave Jesus a holy indignation.

Jesus grew up in the poorest parts of His community in Nazareth, the ghetto. He became poor so that we would be rich (2 Corinthians 8:9). When the thieves distracted their worship, it stirred the holy fire in Jesus to declare from two Old Testament Scriptures in Isaiah 56:7 and Jeremiah 7:11 that "His Father's house would not be a den of robbers, but a house of prayer for ALL the nations." Psalm 69:9 (NASB) says, "Zeal for God's house would consume Him." He could not tolerate people calling the temple (church) His Father's house when He didn't reside there. This consumed Him.

> And Jesus entered the temple and drove out all those who were buying and selling in the temple, and overturned the tables of the moneychangers and the seats of those who were selling doves. And He said to them, "It is written, 'MY HOUSE SHALL BE CALLED A HOUSE OF PRAYER'; but you are making it a ROBBERS' DEN." And *the* blind and *the* lame came to Him in the temple, and He healed them. But when the chief priests and the scribes saw the wonderful things that He had done, and the children who were shouting in the temple, "Hosanna to the Son of David," they became indignant.
>
> —Matthew 21:12-15 NASB

> The chief priests and the scribes heard *this*, and *began* seeking how to destroy Him; for they were afraid of Him, for the whole crowd was astonished at His teaching.
>
> —Mark 11:18 NASB

Observe what happens when Jesus cleanses the temple in verse 14 of Matthew, "and *the* blind and *the* lame came to Him in the temple, and He healed them." Those who needed healing were healed when Jesus showed up at church! ONCE THE CHURCH IS CLEAN FROM SPIRITUAL ABUSE AND ADVERSITY, HEALING CAN TAKE PLACE! *God is raising up prophetic ministries who will stand in righteous boldness against spiritual abuse and oppression. It is time that the people who are innocently trying to worship God can truly encounter hope and healing. We must fight for the broken and hurting in our churches and the world. There is a right time to have a holy indignation for people who are being oppressed.* For example, we should have a holy indignation for the heresy and apostasy of the prosperity gospel, the gospel of universalism, interfaith movements, coexistence, legalism, and liberalism and preach truth and love.

God is a lover of justice and we have to be a voice to the voiceless. As I said earlier, every church building is not God's house and everyone who preaches is not representing God. There is a difference between true shepherds and hirelings (John 10:12-13). TRUTH isn't served at a buffet; it's a delicacy that many have not truly tasted (1 Peter 2:3). And some people just like being lied to. Who's attached to your voice or influence? Whatever influences you will influence your audience. Hopefully it's the unadulterated, untwisted, untainted Word of God!

The vessel may be imperfect, but the Word should cause people to grow in perfection (maturity). *We must have the Heartbeat of a Berean, a Thirst for Truth, a Mindset like a Martyr, and a Determination as a Disciple.*

Where are the contenders of the faith? Read the book of Jude. Who is fighting for the TRUTH of GOD'S WORD in the original languages and context and NOT the doctrines of demons (1 Timothy 4) and traditions of men that make the WORD OF GOD of no effect? STAND YOUR GROUND FOR THE TRUTH OF GOD'S WORD (2 Timothy 4:2-5)! Paul was correct when he wrote to Timothy that the time would come when false doctrine will arise and people would be attracted to it. We are still facing difficult days indeed (2 Timothy 3-4).

We fight for the freedom of those who are bound by religion and the traditions of men. We fight for the lost who need a real encounter with Jesus unto salvation. We must stand in the face of this spiritual adversity like Jesus and fight for the freedom of others so they can truly worship God without restraint. Where are the Spiritual Freedom Fighters? The righteous are to be bold as lions (Proverb 28:1). I know my "to" because I follow Jesus who knew His "to." His "to" is my "to." *Preach the gospel, Heal the brokenhearted, Proclaim release to the captives, Recover sight to the blind, Set free those who are oppressed, and Proclaim the favorable year of the Lord, GRACE!*

If it happens in the church building so be it, but Jesus kept it moving and transformational ministry was taking place outside of the four walls. Jesus said in Matthew 28:18-20 to "make disciples," meaning as you go. As you go through life, who is in your circle of influence that you can simply listen to and share the gospel with? You have to GO first! I'M FOLLOWING JESUS AND NOT THE TRENDS OF THE TEMPLE. *There are so many modern day churches that need a good cleansing!*

> For it is time for judgment to begin with the household of God; and if it begins with us first, what will be the outcome for those who do not obey the gospel of God? AND IF IT IS WITH DIFFICULTY THAT THE RIGHTEOUS IS SAVED, WHAT WILL BECOME OF THE GODLESS MAN AND THE SINNER? Therefore, those also who suffer according to the will of God shall entrust their souls to a faithful Creator in doing what is right.
>
> —1 Peter 4:17-19 NASB

Not everyone was fond of Jesus and we have to be willing to suffer in this same way. *When you stand for* truth, you stand out from the crowd. When you can't fit in, it's because you're called out. When man doesn't speak well of you keep sharing truth (Matthew 5:10-12; Luke 6:26). When your purpose is to be prophetic, you won't be popular.

# CHAPTER 8

## PASSiON

By now I'm sure you have felt my passion for the broken, but more importantly you felt the passion of our Lord and Savior through His Word. *He is my passion.* He went to the greatest length to purchase us back. Jesus stood against so many who hated Him and ridiculed Him for helping and healing people. The religious leaders were afraid of this. Why? It was a method without the law and legalism. It was by means of grace and love. I am not saying that passion is turning tables and exposing pastors and ministries. That wasn't Jesus' focus and neither is it mine. However, He did check them with truth and Scripture and we can do that, but Jesus didn't come for the religious. Jesus was upset because they were using God's house to oppress and bind people. *We must look past the oppressors and have Jesus' passion for people.* Moses confronted Pharaoh for the people (Exodus 5:1). Esther stood for her people for such a time as this (Esther 4:14). Daniel would not defile himself and his young friends would not bow to another God (Daniel 1:1-21, 3:1-30). That's Passion!

When everyone wants to build bigger churches, who will be focused on building people? We must endeavor to be as Biblical as possible.

## DO YOU REALLY WANT TO BE LiKE JESUS?

Many of us have prayed Lord, make me more like You. Lord, I want more of You. Lord, use me. Here I am Jesus. Then, all of a sudden you seem to be facing adversity and chaos. No, what you prayed is to be more like Jesus. Being conformed to the image of Christ will place you in situations where you have to love more, forgive more, and tolerate more because God is making you more like Jesus. Christ embodies every characteristic of God in fullness (Colossians 1:15-20, 2:9-10) and desires for His children to be that same reflection (Genesis 1:27; 1 John 2:6).

Throughout all of the things I have been through in ministry, love and forgiveness have been the greatest tests. I have had to forgive parents, pastors, backstabbers, gossipers and it does not make sense to them or me at times, but "Forgiveness is Supernatural" as R. T. Kendall writes in his book *Total Forgiveness*. You have a peace that they don't have in forgiveness and love. Why? Because you are becoming more like Jesus and He is the Prince of Peace. Your biggest test in being like Jesus will always be with family and the familiar. They know you and know what buttons to push to get a reaction out of you, but you push your love button and keep your peace. *Blessed are the Peacemakers.* We are to live counterculture to the world as Believers. I often tell people that the Beatitudes should "Be Your Attitude." Jesus preached what Kingdom living looks like in Matthew chapters 5-7 in the Sermon on the Mount. Listen to Jesus again in Matthew 5:3-12 (NASB):

"Blessed are the poor in spirit, for theirs is the kingdom of heaven.
"Blessed are those who mourn, for they shall be comforted.
"Blessed are the gentle, for they shall inherit the earth.
"Blessed are those who hunger and thirst for righteousness, for they shall be satisfied.
"Blessed are the merciful, for they shall receive mercy.
"Blessed are the pure in heart, for they shall see God.
"Blessed are the peacemakers, for they shall be called sons of God.
"Blessed are those who have been persecuted for the sake of righteousness, for theirs is the kingdom of heaven.
"Blessed are you when *people* insult you and persecute you, and falsely say all kinds of evil against you because of Me.
"Rejoice and be glad, for your reward in heaven is great; for in the same way they persecuted the prophets who were before you.

It does not make sense to live like this, but it makes for a full life as a Believer. Blessed is interpreted as "fortunate" or "happy" in the Greek. So Jesus gave us an outline for the first *Pursuit of Happyness*.

## LOVE YOUR NEiGHBOR

> Jesus answered, "The foremost is, 'HEAR, O ISRAEL! THE LORD OUR GOD IS ONE LORD; AND YOU SHALL LOVE THE LORD YOUR GOD WITH ALL YOUR HEART, AND WITH ALL YOUR SOUL, AND WITH ALL YOUR MIND, AND WITH ALL YOUR STRENGTH.' "The second is this, 'YOU SHALL LOVE YOUR NEIGHBOR AS YOURSELF.' There is no other commandment greater than these."
>
> —Mark 12:29-31 NASB

Before the young man who called me his pastor moved in next door to me, there was a couple with three children that lived there. We spoke sporadically in passing. Then the fights would start. He and his girlfriend would be yelling and screaming at one another. One day it sounded like furniture was moving, the walls were shaking, and they woke up my whole family early in the morning. I was going to call the police, which I avoided in previous fights because I did not want to endanger my family in his retaliation. So I went to their house and asked him what was the problem. He apologized for the fighting and said she was beating him, which was evident. He said they have fallen on really hard times financially; he couldn't find work and had no car. Then he started crying about it and I shared how we lost our house to foreclosure and was unemployed many times with a family. I said as a man I know how hard it was to be the provider in these economic times. I asked if he was a believer and he said yes, and then thanked me for coming to talk to him.

Another day a fight was happening around 1:30 A.M. and my wife and I were downstairs and I was just tired of it. I kept saying I was going to call the police, but I didn't want him taken away from his family again. So I knocked on his front door and he said, "Sorry neighbor not now." I said, "Yes now. You all are waking up my family. What is going on?" He came out and told me how his dad abandoned him and he was fighting to stay together with his girlfriend and they wanted to get married. He just cried and bared his soul. I put my arm on his shoulder and said I'm here for you man. He said, "thank you neighbor." I told him I know you want your family, but you can't let these problems rob you from your peace and let your babies see this fighting. You all are turning against each other and need to turn towards each other. My wife was talking to his girlfriend at the same time and they both really loved each other, but problems got the best of them. Mind you, this was the last night right before they were being evicted. He didn't care because he didn't like the neighborhood anyway. We extended help for whatever they needed, but they refused. We did offer them a "DRAMA FREE" t-shirt (which they accepted) from our BIGWO shirt line with Scriptures on the back ranging from avoiding foolish talk, sexual immorality, pride, etc. so they would remember us and that the Word in you keeps you DRAMA FREE. We prayed with them, and they felt the sense of hope and eventually moved, but what I recalled from this is that he always called me "neighbor." I told him my name many times, but he just kept calling me neighbor.

We have wanted to move out of this neighborhood for so long and still desire that for the safety of our family, but him calling me neighbor numerous times sparked purpose and passion in me to be salt and light (Matthew

5:13-16) in the hopeless neighborhood. The Word was really becoming manifested for us to be more like Jesus. We had an outreach in our neighborhood weeks later to feed people, have fun for the kids, preach the gospel, pray for them and give them hope. People gave their lives to Christ; some even came to the church, but what I saw happening in our church was the Word becoming manifested to them. We were being more like Jesus. We were actually being the church.

We had two of our leaders give their testimonies of who they were before and after Christ at the outreach. Dominic talked about his dad not being in his life and how God has become His Father, which was good for the males to hear and know that Daddy adopts you. Norah used drugs very young and thought that this was normal life for everyone. After she shared her story she began praying for the people with addictions and the tears began to fall because she could feel the compassion for those still using drugs, knowing God delivered her from that. She was reflecting on her encounter with the Most High God where she found FORGIVENESS AT THE FEET OF JESUS.

She was telling her redemption story. Then the members of the church were crying because they had never experienced being in a neighborhood, being Christ in the earth offering faith, hope, and love. Some of them had been in church for years and had never been part of an outreach. As a young church plant, the majority of the content in this book has been taught over the years, but they realized this is what Discipleship looks like in Scripture. Being the church. It's not the building that makes the church, but the people who are the church! It's one thing to preach a sermon series at Remnant called chURch (you are the church), but it is more imperative to implement the Acts 2:41-47 reality.

## GET DiRTY

This is what Christianity is all about! Loving like Christ, Living like Christ, and Leading like Christ. He didn't take on our sins, die on the cross, rise from the dead and appear to over 500 people for us to sit in an air conditioned worship center, warm pews, drink coffee and have an hour and fifteen minute service (or longer) and call that church. We check the box and think we have done God a favor. That's American Christianity. WE NEED TO GET DIRTY! We need to smell like sheep, tend to the sheep, and feed His sheep (John 21:15-17). That's Biblical Christianity! Stop being afraid to GET DIRTY for Jesus, HE GOT DIRTY FOR US. He washed the Disciples feet and said for us to Serve One Another and Love One Another just as He did in John 13:14-15, 34-35:

> "If I then, the Lord and the Teacher, washed your feet, you also ought to wash one another's feet. For I gave you an example that you also should do as I did to you."

> "A new commandment I give to you, that you love one another, even as I have loved you, that you also love one another. By this all men will know that you are My disciples, if you have love for one another."

Have you ever really washed someone's feet or had yours washed? It's humbling for both parties. I would challenge husbands and wives to literally wash each other's feet, parents and children, pastors and leaders. It is a sign of the humility of Jesus. I am not suggesting doing this literally that often, but to take the posture of Jesus and lovingly serve everyone in your life, especially if you are a leader. Jesus was a servant leader. SO GET DIRTY.

My prayer for this book is that more Christians would become dirty, not in the *sin sense*, but in the *sense of serving*. Remember people outside of the church are Attracted to Authenticity. They want to know why you love Jesus. Why should they give their life to a God when they don't see you benefit from having faith in Him? They need to see you are not a perfect little Christian afraid of sinners, but a Believer who can lead them to truth and transformation in Christ. People are looking for hope, looking for something to believe in, and looking for love in all the wrong places. What if they didn't have to search for it much longer and we showed up with the answer? It is In Christ Alone. Anthony Evans sang an awesome rendition of "In Christ Alone" and I pray these lyrics bless you.

**"In Christ Alone"**

*In Christ alone my hope is found*
*He is my light my strength my song*
*This Cornerstone, this solid Ground*
*Firm through the fiercest drought and storm*
*What heights of love, what depths of peace*
*When fears are stilled when strivings cease!*
*My Comforter my All in All*
*Here in the love of Christ I stand*

*In Christ alone!—who took on flesh*
*Fullness of God in helpless babe!*
*This Gift of love and righteousness*
*Scorned by the ones He came to save*

*Till on that cross as Jesus died*
*The wrath of God was satisfied*
*For every sin on Him was laid*
*Here in the death of Christ I live*

*There in the ground His body lay*
*Light of the world by darkness slain*
*Then bursting forth in glorious Day*
*Up from the grave He rose again!*
*And as He stands in victory*
*Sin's curse has lost its grip on me*
*For I am His and He is mine*
*Bought with the precious blood of Christ*

*No guilt in life no fear in death*
*This is the power of Christ in me*
*From life's first cry to final breath*
*Jesus commands my destiny*
*No power of hell no scheme of man*
*Can ever pluck me from His hand*
*Till he returns or calls me home*
*Here in the power of Christ I'll stand!*

# CHAPTER 9

## DADDY'S LOVE

Until we can understand the love of God for ourselves, we won't be convinced or confident to fulfill the Great Commission. It's hard to love your neighbor as yourself if you don't love yourself or know God loves you. *Crazy Love* by Francis Chan is a great book on God's relentless love for us. It was an inspiration to meet him and you can discern he truly walks in the humility of Christ. I respect a man who didn't want his church to be as big as possible, but as biblical as possible. But if you never pick up his book, pick up the Bible.

I love what Misty Edwards and Jesus Culture sing in the song "You Won't Relent." "You won't relent until You have it all. My heart is Yours." GOD WANTS OUR HEART BEFORE WE DO ONE THING FOR HIM. And He wants it EVEN more after we are busy in ministry. OUR INTIMACY WITH HIM WILL BE THE SOURCE THAT SUSTAINS AND STRENGTHENS US! Remember, before Jesus did anything for His call He knew the Father was pleased with Him. It's something about *knowing Daddy is for you*

(Romans 8:31) that gives you a determination to fulfill your destiny.

Throughout all the pain that I grew up in with my parents, I always wanted my dad to approve of me. I think that is in every child. There is nothing like a father's touch and embrace. And then on the flip side when you're abandoned or abused, you search for that touch through many avenues. Even though there was much strife in our family from my dad's narcissism and mom's bitterness, and my parent's public divorce locally and nationally, God has brought great healing to and through me. But my eyes were often distracted on the wrong daddy. I had to know my Daddy in heaven loved me. And because I didn't always feel that from my dad, I felt that God must not love me like that either.

I have a very close friend named Bryan, who I consider a brother. We love spending time together with our families. Whenever we would go through great tribulation in life they were always our safe haven and vice versa. I remember our families praying together at their house and he started off the prayer with "Daddy." I was like, who is this dude talking to? Is he calling God Daddy? Who does that? Whatever.

He has a strong prophetic gift and is very in tune with the heart and voice of God and is often looked at as weird, but anyone with a prophetic call is most likely to be viewed as such. However, the "Daddy Prayer" made my soul search for a deeper relationship so I could know Him as Daddy.

> For you have not received a spirit of slavery leading to fear again, but you have received a spirit of adoption as sons by which we cry out, "Abba! Father!" The Spirit Himself testifies with our spirit that we are children of God, and if children, heirs also, heirs of God and fellow heirs with Christ, if indeed we suffer with *Him* so that we may also be glorified with *Him.*
>
> —Romans 8:15-17 NASB

## SONSHiP

I used to think my problems with not knowing who I was in Christ was because of sin in my life, but it wasn't. I DIDN'T KNOW I WAS HIS SON! O, for us to know that we can cry out "Abba!" "Daddy!" "Papa!" My friend's parents were divorced too, he was familiar with family pain, related to religious manipulation and shared in spiritual abuse too, but he made it out because he knew he was Daddy's son. My problem wasn't my sin or the shame of standing before the church, it was SONSHIP! Once again it was reading and believing Daddy at His Word that caused another encounter for my transformation.

> For if we have become united with *Him* in the likeness of His death, certainly we shall also be *in the likeness* of His resurrection, knowing this, that our old self was crucified with *Him,* in order that our body of sin might be done away with, so that we would no longer be slaves to sin; for he who has died is freed from sin. Now if we have died with Christ, we believe that we shall also live with Him, knowing that Christ, having been raised from the dead, is never to die again; death no longer is master over Him. For the death that He died, He died to sin once for all; but the life that He lives, He lives to God. Even so consider yourselves to be dead to sin, but alive to God in Christ Jesus. Therefore do not let sin reign in your mortal body so that you obey its lusts, and do not go on presenting the members of your body to sin *as* instruments of unrighteousness; but present yourselves to God as those alive from the dead, and your members *as* instruments of righteousness to God. For sin shall not be master over you, for you are not under law but under grace.
> —Romans 6:5-14 NASB

Sin has no dominion over us! OUR PROBLEM IS NOT WITH SIN IT'S SONSHIP! The Son of God dealt with the Power and Penalty of sin on the Cross, so that God the Father would adopt us and the Holy Spirit of God reminds us that we are HIS! IT IS FINISHED! THAT SETTLES THE SIN ISSUE. SIN WAS THE PROBLEM, SONSHIP WAS THE SOLUTION! The Law makes you feel condemned, not God. Grace sets you free! If you are in Christ you are His.

> Therefore there is now no condemnation for those who are in Christ Jesus. For the law of the Spirit of life in Christ Jesus has set you free from the law of sin and of death. For what the Law could not do, weak as it was through the flesh, God *did:* sending His own Son in the likeness of sinful flesh and *as an offering* for sin, He condemned sin in the flesh, so that the requirement of the Law might be fulfilled in us, who do not walk according to the flesh but according to the Spirit.
>
> —Romans 8:1-4 NASB

Once you can understand SONSHIP, the shackles of shame and abuse will fall off. Every family stronghold can be broken. Let the truth that you are free from sin by HIS GRACE release you to the arms of Daddy. The sweet embrace of the Holy Spirit will remind you in the secret times YOU ARE MY CHILD AND I LOVE YOU (Romans 8:16)!

GOD LOVES US FROM THE INSIDE OUT. You don't have to know every scripture to come to God before He is pleased. You don't have to have a three-piece suit or church dress on to look holy. You don't need be like anybody in church, but Jesus. YOU ARE FREE FROM SIN! You are free because of Jesus! You couldn't do anything about it but receive and believe. Receive your freedom now! Receive it in the name of Jesus. WHOM THE SON SETS FREE IS FREE INDEED (John 8:35-36)! You are free! Kierra Sheard's title track "Free" is one of the most powerful worship songs I have ever heard. The ministry in this song has literally caused people to be touched by the presence of God instantly during our worship services.

**"Free"**

*My redeemer has saved me from sin*
*My soul is awakened, I live*
*Free from what held me, Free from what fought me*
*Mentally, You've captured me*
*In my mind, I am free, In my heart, If I am Yours*
*I am free*
*(Repeat)*

*Where the Spirit of the Lord our God is at rest there is freedom*
*You can be freed from bondage and healed from brokenness and full of joy*
*Be free . . .*
*(Repeat)*

*Be free from the bitterness in your heart (Be Free)*

*Be free from the dysfunctional relationship (Be Free)*

*You can be freed from bondage and healed from brokenness and full of joy*

*Be from what mama and daddy did to you (Be Free)*

*Be free from whatever it is that you went through behind closed doors (Be Free)*

*You can be freed from bondage and healed from brokenness and full of joy*

*Be free from whatever demon you're wrestling with (Be Free)*

*You can Be free from whatever it is you're going through . . . (Be Free)*

*Kierra's Prayer . . .*

*I come against every witch, warlock, every demon that is not like God. I come against every force that is not like the God almighty that I serve. And I speak the blood of Jesus against every attack, against every plan, against every spirit that is not like God. For He has given us the power. He has not given us the spirit of fear, but of Power! And of love, and a sound mind. I gotta sound mind. I speak it in the atmosphere. It doesn't matter what I'm going through I am free. I am free! I'm free! Anybody believe that you're free. You can act like you got it all together if you want to. But the devil he works . . . but I know a Man named Jesus. He is the Living Word. There's POWER in Jesus! There's Healing in Jesus. Woman you can be healed. You can be healed. You can be set free. You don't gotta be an alcoholic like mama and daddy was . . . you don't have to be a crackhead . . . I come against every generational curse in the Name of Jesus. Be Free! I speak freedom in the atmosphere. You can see yourself reaching your best ability, your best potential. You can see yourself breaking the curse and birthing something new in your bloodline. Anybody want to be free? Lift your hands and show the devil you are free. This is our sign of surrenderence to You Oh God. We want to be free from homosexuality. We don't want to be like this Oh God. We don't want to have the lustful desires. We want to free from fornication. We want to be free from suicidal thoughts. We want to be free. I cry out for every individual that's in this room. We want to be free Oh God. You show Yourself strong in this room. I believe the God that I read about, the God that I pray to, the God that I sing about. He can break chains in the spiritual ream. And God I say yes You have Your way. We welcome You in this place. We want to be free. We want to be more like You . . .*

## PROPHETiC PHONE CALLS

My friend Bryan would randomly call me in the past and say, "Daddy Loves You." I would say, "Yeah I know." He would say it again until I believed it and the transformation began years ago. He recently texted me and shared the same thing. I had to pull back from life and ministry and receive it again and again. With the prophetic call on his life it was not a condemning word, a word of judgment or even that I will be blessed financially, but that Yahweh, The Most High God, The Lord, The God of All Creation, Abba, My Daddy LOVES me. Yes you too!

It was the same prophetic call and confirmation that embodied the person of Jesus Christ. GOD LOVES

US. Exemplifying that God sent Me here because of Love (John 3:16-17). GOD IS LOVE. If we never receive "a word" from another prophet, Jesus is our Prophet, Priest, and King. He is God! He is Love! He is Truth! He is Grace! These are not just words in the Bible, they are Him. He is the Logos, the Word (John 1:1). *He Preached, Practiced, and Personified the POWER OF LOVE.* The Word of God is our prophetic word that Daddy's Love Us!

> Beloved, let us love one another, for love is from God; and everyone who loves is born of God and knows God. The one who does not love does not know God, for God is love.
>
> —1 John 4:7-8 NASB

## LEARNiNG LOVE

I told my wife early on in our marriage that I loved her, and I surely believed I did and she honestly said in that moment, "No you don't, you're learning to love me." Ouch! I thought to myself how could you stay with someone who you know doesn't really love you the way you deserve? God was using Chrystal to teach me God's love even more. LOVE IS A LEARNING PROCESS. Learning to Love God, yourself, and your neighbor. You have to sit down in the class of life with Jesus and begin the process of LEARNING LOVE. When we learn to love like Jesus we become mature. Bryan was helping me grow up in love. You want to be like Jesus right? In the greatest love chapter in the Bible, 1 Corinthians 13 where you see "Love," put God there (God is patient, God is kind). Then if you pray to really be like Jesus, put your name there (Warren is patient, Warren is kind). Once you grasp this you can discover the truth of verse 11 and declare I'm not a child anymore in regards to loving. God's Love matures us.

"If I speak with the tongues of men and of angels, but do not have love, I have become a noisy gong or a clanging cymbal. If I have *the gift of* prophecy, and know all mysteries and all knowledge; and if I have all faith, so as to remove mountains, but do not have love, I am nothing. And if I give all my possessions to feed *the poor,* and if I surrender my body to be burned, but do not have love, it profits me nothing. Love is patient, love is kind *and* is not jealous; love does not brag *and* is not arrogant, does not act unbecomingly; it does not seek its own, is not provoked, does not take into account a wrong *suffered,* does not rejoice in unrighteousness, but rejoices with the truth; bears all things, believes all things, hopes all things, endures all things. Love never fails; but if *there are gifts of* prophecy, they will be done away; if *there are* tongues, they will cease; if *there is* knowledge, it will be done away. For we know in part and we prophesy in part;

but when the perfect comes, the partial will be done away. When I was a child, I used to speak like a child, think like a child, reason like a child; when I became a man, I did away with childish things. For now we see in a mirror dimly, but then face to face; now I know in part, but then I will know fully just as I also have been fully known. But now faith, hope, love, abide these three; but the greatest of these is love."

—1 Corinthians 13:1-13 NASB

As a music lover, songwriter, and artist, music becomes the soundtrack to our lives, and my inspiration to write songs have to be lived through the Word of God and life experiences; which is probably why this book is so autobiographical. If I can't show you how the Word of God is my source of authority in my life then I can't authentically preach, write or share anything. Application is the truest form of Biblical interpretation.

My first album was called *"When I Was A Child,"* where I was at the place of still LEARNING LOVE. This project was written from my family pain and hurt derived from church members as I was in the search for healing, which set up the second album, which you know as *"Follow After Love."* This is based on the first verse of 1 Corinthians 14 in the American Standard Version:

Follow after love; yet desire earnestly spiritual *gifts*, but rather that ye may prophesy.

—1 Corinthians 14:1 ASV

### *"Follow After Love"*

*Verse 1*
*So much older now, ain't got it figured it out*
*But I know my place, it's standing in His grace*
*Got the shoulders now, I can bear it how*
*Cause I call His name and I seek His face*
*In the times of ignorance, did not reciprocate His Love*
*Didn't know love had a difference, my definition was so numb*
*That's before I could understand that His love does not condemn*
*And the same love that has covered me is the same love free to them*
*So I follow after love*

*Hook*
*I follow after Love cause Love came after me*
*When I was bound in chains Your Love set me free*
*I don't fear no more, You have so much in store*
*Your Love changed my life and I'm Your vessel to pour*

*Verse 2*
*So many haters now, but Your Love works them out*
*Don't have to prove my place, people pleasing erased*
*Got perspective now, I can share it how*
*Cause You set the pace and finished the race*
*Got the confidence of my call and the courage to pursue*
*Edify the Body of Christ and prophesy to them in truth*

*Mature Love unconditionally no image of formality*
*And the same love that has covered me flows down from Calvary*
*So I follow after Love*

*Rap*
*Put away them childish things*
*Now my life's full circle like a wedding ring*
*Haters got their eyes on me, but I got mine set on Eternal things*
*Everything else is vanity, not worried about this world and calamity*
*Things about to be added to me, but I'm huge target for the enemy*
*Attacks on my life and family, but Love is the sign that He lives in me*
*So I'm a keep pursuing His Love for me, won't be separated for eternity*

I had learned to mature in love. I have not arrived, but I am not the same broken person rehearsing my pain and feeling like God abandoned me. I am *following after love* and learning to give what I have received to all. I know I am His son on this album. Also, Paul tells us in the context of 1 Corinthians 14 that they were desiring spiritual gifts, but it was better that they prophesy in understanding to bring edification to unbelievers.

My friend prophesied to me about God's love. It was simple and he made sure I understood it, but the depth of God's love is so immeasurable that we will still be in awe even in heaven.

This song I wrote articulates my process from wanting to know God's love, then receiving and reciprocating Daddy's love.

### *"I Love You Jesus"*

*Verse 1*
*Reflecting on my sinful ways. Death the wages that I paid.*
*Thinking I'm not worthy of amazing grace (I can't stand to see my face)*
*Not knowing what Your true love is, wrong perception as a kid.*
*Thought I had to perform for You. But all You want is a heart that's true.*
*The search is on to fill my void. Now damaged like old Christmas toys.*
*Here I am broken and bent, with this cruel world my time is spent*
*In my life can true love begin?*
*Even though I'm full of sin?*
*I just wanna know who I can put my trust in?*

*Hook*
*(1ˢᵗ full chorus—I wanna know you Jesus)*
*I, I, I, I Love you Jesus, I Love Jesus*
*Cause you first Loved me (echo)*
*Cause you died for me (echo)*
*I, I, I, I really Love you Jesus, I Love Jesus*
*Cause you first Loved me (echo)*
*And you rose for me (echo)*

*Verse 2*
*I'm grateful now for what you did. You paid the price for all my sins.*
*My past you won't bring up again. Your words are grace inheritance.*

*It was Your love that lifted me, carried me, protected me, set me free.*
*And all I had to do was believe*
*Your love is not performance based, because of love I will obey.*
*You healed my pain and took my shame, stripped the power of sinful reign.*
*Guilty on my way to hell, but I gotta love story to tell.*
*Of your unconditional love that never fails . . . me*

*Bridge*
*You created us from out of dust, then turned us over to sinful lust*
*Shed your blood, now saved by grace, justified because of faith*
*Forever your name will I praise, when I boldly come to seek your face*
*I offer you my heart always and I just really wanna say*
*You are love, You are grace; My sinful image has been replaced*
*Now I'm a new creation, You are my propitiation*
*I worship you and give you praise, I offer you my heart always*
*And all I really wanna say is . . .*

*Hook*

*Outro*
*Broken and bitter I was so damaged*
*I was so angry and confused*
*I didn't know how to love like You*
*But you showed me through Mercy*
*Showed me through Grace*
*I just want to seek your face*
*I'm forever grateful to You*
*Daddy I am grateful to You*

I want to prophecy to you, DADDY LOVES YOU! I pray that His Love edifies you every day of your life. LEARN TO LOVE your families the way you may not have been loved. As I said early, there is nothing like the Father's embrace. My eldest son Josiah is a big love bug. He will hug you all day if you let him. At times, I really was not given a lot of affection from my dad in my adolescent years and in turn, I wasn't really affectionate to my sons as they began to grow older. My middle son Micaiah hugs you when he feels like it and my baby girl Kaira of course gets much affection from daddy.

However, because of my brokenness I almost couldn't stand hugs from my sons. I've learned now that if I don't give them the father's embrace, they may be on the same search I was on thinking my heavenly Father didn't love me. Praise God for Practice. Learning to Love means action and time to children. So Micaiah even loves hugging now. Before going to bed the other day Josiah said to his mom, "I feel so good when daddy hugs me." This is the same feeling God wants us to receive and reciprocate. And here's the reality, LEARNING TO LOVE LIKE HIM IS A LIFE LONG PROCESS. Embrace it as He embraces you.

# CHAPTER 10

## TELL YOUR STORY

The inspiration for this book arose from the story of a woman deemed a sinner by reputation, dirty by religious denomination and unworthy by occupation, Mary of Bethany. Everywhere the gospel was to be preached, what this woman did would be told as a memorial to her. I didn't hear this celebration close in the Baptist church, "She washed, she wiped, she kissed and she anointed Jesus' feet." I just heard, "He died on a Friday, laid in a borrowed tomb all day Saturday, but early, I said early Sunday morning! He got up with all power in His hands!" Yes that's His story, but Mary had a story too.

As I read the gospels and her story time and again, I felt as if Mary was left out of the gospel message. So my search was on to discover this significant event that Jesus said was supposed to be told everywhere the gospel was preached.

They didn't want her there. She was "dirty" in their eyes. They didn't want Jesus to touch her because He would get "dirty." But what she did was so significant for Jesus' sacrifice and burial *He said* to include it in the gospel message (Matthew 26:13; Mark 14:9). I started to see myself in the text. In no way am I diminishing the work of Calvary's Cross—I am suggesting that I found a story that was lost. We may preach that He got up early, but *she got down humbly.* We know that Jesus said, "Father forgive them for they know not what they do (Luke 23:34)," but *He forgave her so gently in front of her accusers.* We know that the church began when Joel 2:28 was confirmed on the Day of Pentecost and the Holy Spirit was poured out on all flesh (Acts 2), but *Mary poured out her expensive oil for Jesus first.*

We serve a God who wants us to TELL OUR REDEMPTION STORY. We serve a God who wasn't worried about getting "dirty." We serve a God who stooped down to raise sinners up. That's my Lord and Savior. The God of the universe was not afraid of the dirt that He made us from. What do I mean? Not our sin, He wasn't afraid to go get His children back that were made from dirt (Genesis 1:26) and strayed from His arms. What a loving Father we have. Without the Spirit of God, all we are is dirt (Genesis 2:7).

Mary was my inspiration to search the Scriptures and see how many people encountered this gentle Jesus who was full of grace and truth, love and life, peace and power and recount the endless people who could not keep quiet about the gospel of the Kingdom that changed their lives forever.

One of our greatest Apostles was struck by Jesus because the Lord didn't see Saul as "too dirty" to be called by Him to preach the gospel. Jesus was so concerned with Paul that He appeared to Him after His ascension. And Paul never forgot to *tell his redemption story* (Acts 26), which is why many people were won to the Lord through the power of the gospel and the power of his authenticity. Paul talked about who he was before Christ, a murderer of Christians, how religious and pious he could be as a religious leader (Philippians 3), what he struggled with after Christ (Romans 7), but that his strength only came from Christ (Philippians 4:13). He walked in humility with believers and unbelievers and still saw himself as a "dirty Christian," but he was confident in His call:

> "I thank Christ Jesus our Lord, who has strengthened me, because He considered me faithful, putting me into service, even though I was formerly a blasphemer and a persecutor

and a violent aggressor. Yet I was shown mercy because I acted ignorantly in unbelief; and the grace of our Lord was more than abundant, with the faith and love which are *found* in Christ Jesus. It is a trustworthy statement, deserving full acceptance, that Christ Jesus came into the world to save sinners, among whom I am foremost *of all.* Yet for this reason I found mercy, so that in me as the foremost, Jesus Christ might demonstrate His perfect patience as an example for those who would believe in Him for eternal life. Now to the King eternal, immortal, invisible, the only God, *be* honor and glory forever and ever. Amen."

—1 Timothy 1:12-17 NASB

Paul said I am the "foremost of all sinners." In other words, I was the "dirtiest" one. But what does God do? Take the most unruly, unexpected, and unlikely ones and lavishes His rich mercy on them. It's what I call a "W.H.A.T." moment, "Watch Him Anoint Them!" The troublemakers, tattooed, weird, and wayward are "the foolish ones who confound the wise" (1 Corinthians 1:27). That is what our reaction will be when the unlikely are called by God. "WHAT?!" Some people need a W.H.A.T. moment to happen in their lives.

Jesus Christ demonstrates His divine purpose through Dirty Christianity. Yes, we are New Creatures in Christ. The old has passed away (2 Corinthians 5:17), but none of us are squeaky clean perfect parishioners. We are prone to the presence of sin as long as we are in this flesh. Thanks be to God that the power and penalty of sin was eradicated on the Cross of Christ. One of my mentors said, "God put what He loved the most and hated the most on the cross at the same time." God had to punish our sin so we would never feel His wrath, but He loved His only begotten Son simultaneously. That is the good news because it should have been us. HE IS OUR PROPITIATION (Hebrews 2:17; 1 John 2:2, 4:10).

## TRANSFORMATiONAL TESTiMONiES

It often amazes me how the world can take a Biblical concepts and benefit tremendously from the implemented principles. We often stray from the powerful traditions that do make the Word of God effective. For example, the world donates money to charitable organizations all the time, which is the principle of sowing and reaping and is very beneficial during tax season (Luke 6:38; 2 Corinthians 9:6). Many in the world write their visions out for businesses, goals, and dreams (Proverbs 16:3, 19; Habakkuk 2:2). The world has many programs that mentor kids where someone helps shape their future so they can be a better person (James 1:27). That is discipleship. I discovered another Biblical or church principle relating to the context of telling your story used is in the world of health and fitness, particularly through the success story of P90X.

## P90X

We all have seen the late night infomercials that have been running for years where Tony Horton is telling you this program is for you. I took the plunge a few years ago and can boast on completing 3.5 rounds of P90X with over 50 pounds of weight loss. Bring it baby! "X" That's my TRANSFORMATIONAL TESTIMONY. It was hard, I wanted to quit, but being healthy for my family was my inspiration to keep pushing. They tell you to decide, commit, and succeed. But P90X is not successful because the program is great for overall fitness or that Tony is in his mid fifties and is highly motivational or that the nutrition guide is the best for your dietary needs. So why is it so successful?

I read that their success sporadically increased because people committing to the 90-day program began to send their BEFORE AND AFTER photo results to Beach Body (the parent company of P90X). Once they started receiving ordinary people's transformation pictures they included them in the infomercial and the product flew off the shelves. The people were showing that the product (i.e. JESUS) was worth committing to, and the results didn't lie that transformation has taken place. People were preaching the gospel or good news of P90X. Hmm . . . Who was I before Christ and after Christ. Maybe we need to show some photos to display in our churches. When I read this info about P90X I said, they got it!

Maybe we as the church can revisit the old school secret to P90X's success. Because we are still trying to convince people that Jesus, His gospel, and His love are relevant without unbelievers seeing the RESULTS of OUR PRODUCT; our faith working. Without our TRANSFORMATIONAL TESTIMONIES people are not convinced that He's a God worth committing to. But the truth is, TRANSFORMATIONAL TESTIMONIES were always OUR PRODUCT'S POWERFUL SUCCESS STORY too.

## EJM

Eddie James Ministries is an intercessory, praise and worship, dance, rap, and arts ministry to young people who are broken through drugs, abuse, addictions, cutting, homosexuality, gangs, pornography, etc. Eddie James, who is a Phoenix native, singer, songwriter, musician, minister, and spiritual father, takes these kids around the nation and world to spread the gospel of Jesus Christ through the arts. The music is powerful and full of the Presence of God with sound theological lyrics. The dancers are so good they could compete on *MTV's* *"America's Best Dance Crew."* The Presence of God that enters the atmosphere when they minister leaves you in awe, but the presentation is just a set up for the real reason why they tirelessly tour throughout the year. These tattooed, pierced, gifted and eclectic religion rejects from all ethnic backgrounds are not there to entertain the masses alone. Their purpose is to speak of Transformation through the Power of the Holy Spirit.

We have witnessed The Holy Spirit set this part of the service up perfectly every time. A pause comes over the audience just before the real ministry begins. Eddie will choose a group of young men or women to share their Transformational Testimonies of who they once were before finding Jesus and becoming free from their bondage by the love of Jesus. The Holy Spirit knows exactly who is in the crowd and desperately needs to hear the exact "dirty" story of redemption by Divine appointment every night. While those in the crowd are facing the inner doubting question, "Can I ever change?" They connect to the story then a shift happens. Eddie has those giving their Transformational Testimony shift into praying for hope, healing, deliverance and freedom for any young people who might be struggling with the same sin and strongholds that once had them bound. It is one of the most powerful moments I have ever witnessed through young people.

EJM embraces these young people and gives them a home of healing, a life on the road in ministry where he trains them to have a strong prayer life, teaches them the Word of God, and allows them to express themselves in a way that some church folk would say "it doesn't take all that." And the results are solid. These young people are being used for the glory of God while some in the church still haven't embraced the arts. The reason so many young people are selling themselves for the riches of the world is because it allows every gift and talent to be expressed, while the church has not been the safe haven to heal brokenness and then let the healed individuals use their gifts to share the gospel. At one time, Eddie James Ministries traveled with 65 young people around the nation and world all year long.

One night during an Eddie James revival held at Remnant, a young man who was a part of our church was struggling with homosexuality and heard a TRANSFORMATIONAL TESTIMONY of another young man named Kegan who was raped by several men at a birthday party and later by a woman. This caused him to be addicted to drugs, abuse alcohol and have bisexual relationships trying to find love and affirmation. He said he would cry in his bed and didn't want to be gay, and met Jesus at an Eddie James concert and Jesus set him free from that bondage! He spoke about the reality of his FREEDOM AND RESPONSIBILITY to live a godly life. This was so relevant because he was saying yes I am free from this, but I must make the right choices and be responsible to stay free. This caused the young man of our church to leave his current lifestyle, depart from Phoenix two days later, and he is now on the road to new life in Christ and was a part of the ministry with EJM. All because someone was not ashamed to share their story. *HIStory always changes our story for His glory. When you are truly free, you will be free to share your Gospel Redemption Story.*

## WHERE iS YOUR DAMASCUS?

In 2006, a guest preacher came to speak at my dad's church and it changed my life forever. Pastor CJ Blair was not your typical preacher. I remember seeing his picture sent by his church and thought we were in for something very different. I thought this dude looks like he is about to wreck the church, literally. But this man preached the Word of God with such power and force that my soul was stirring. I couldn't stay in my seat and kept telling my friend next to me that my stomach was spinning. It was the call of God resonating in me that this was the liberating power of the gospel I had read about in my dad's church and desired to experience. It was happening in my home church right before my eyes. This man then told his story!

His mother was a former prostitute, his father abandoned him, he was in and out of jail since he was a juvenile and then became a drug dealer. Then he had a Damascus experience in his car. The Lord spoke to him by name and said, "CJ" and he replied, "Yes Lord." He shared that he thought he was going to die and God just lets you know He's real before He kills you. God told him to stop listening to the hip-hop music and then told him to throw the drugs out of the car. CJ put his hands up and began worshipping God. He eventually went home and went to Bible College a changed man. He later saw the drug dealer (whose drugs he threw away) in a barbershop and he thought he was going to kill him. He said I heard you're with the Lord now and ask to pray for him then left. God always protects His children who are called according to His purpose.

His story had the church captivated. We had never heard someone go through so much and survive. That's remnant! You survive to help others live for Christ. By the way, he pastored The Remnant Church and we had not planted Church of The Remnant until a year later, but God had spoken the name to me in the year 2001. What a confirmation for the vision God placed in me that was stirring while he was preaching. But CJ was the pastor of The Remnant Church of C.O.F.A.T. Ministries, with the acronym meaning, "Come Out From Among Them" based on 2 Corinthians 6:17-18 (NASB), "Therefore, COME OUT FROM THEIR MIDST AND BE SEPARATE," says the Lord. "AND DO NOT TOUCH WHAT IS UNCLEAN; And I will welcome you. "And I will be a father to you, And you shall be sons and daughters to Me," Says the Lord Almighty.

God told CJ that he was still in a gang and he said, "Lord, but I'm not bangin' anymore." He told him he was in the church gang, referring to the religious system and denominations. They dressed him up in the three-piece suits, taught him how to play church, and God wanted him to come out from among that. Come out from among them, the modern day Pharisees!

WHERE IS YOUR DAMASCUS? What I love about God is that He is not afraid of how "dirty" we are, because *there is no sin more potent than the precious blood of Jesus.* He knows every sin, mistake, every hidden thing about us. He is Omniscient, All Knowing. Don't be afraid to repent and confess your sin to Him. God is not afraid of the distance He needs to go to get us. The reality is He's always with us. He is Omnipresent, All Pervasive, constantly encountered. It is our own condemnation that makes us feel far from God. Don't be afraid of His voice and return to the Father. God is not afraid of the darkness in our lives (Psalm 139). His light is more powerful then any demonic power and dark place in your life. He is Omnipotent, All Powerful! Don't be afraid if His light exposes places, He is only leading you closer to Him to be a Father to you. He knows all about us, He knows every place we've been, and every place we are going. He is a Sovereign God!

Psalm 139 (NASB)

O LORD, You have searched me and known *me.*
You know when I sit down and when I rise up;
You understand my thought from afar.
You scrutinize my path and my lying down,
And are intimately acquainted with all my ways.
Even before there is a word on my tongue,
Behold, O LORD, You know it all.
You have enclosed me behind and before,
And laid Your hand upon me.
*Such* knowledge is too wonderful for me;
It is *too* high, I cannot attain to it.

Where can I go from Your Spirit?
Or where can I flee from Your presence?
If I ascend to heaven, You are there;
If I make my bed in Sheol, behold, You are there.
If I take the wings of the dawn,
If I dwell in the remotest part of the sea,
Even there Your hand will lead me,
And Your right hand will lay hold of me.
If I say, "Surely the darkness will overwhelm me,
And the light around me will be night,"
Even the darkness is not dark to You,
And the night is as bright as the day.
Darkness and light are alike *to You.*

For You formed my inward parts;
You wove me in my mother's womb.
I will give thanks to You, for I am fearfully and wonderfully made;
Wonderful are Your works,
And my soul knows it very well.
My frame was not hidden from You,
When I was made in secret,
*And* skillfully wrought in the depths of the earth;
Your eyes have seen my unformed substance;
And in Your book were all written
The days that were ordained *for me,*
When as yet there was not one of them.

How precious also are Your thoughts to me, O God!
How vast is the sum of them!
If I should count them, they would outnumber the sand.
When I awake, I am still with You.

O that You would slay the wicked, O God;
Depart from me, therefore, men of bloodshed.
For they speak against You wickedly,
And Your enemies take *Your name* in vain.
Do I not hate those who hate You, O LORD?
And do I not loathe those who rise up against You?
I hate them with the utmost hatred;
They have become my enemies.

Search me, O God, and know my heart;
Try me and know my anxious thoughts;

And see if there be any hurtful way in me,
And lead me in the everlasting way.

GOD KNOWS EXACTLY WHO WE ARE, WHAT DIRT WE'VE DONE AND WHAT WE ARE PRONE TO DO, BUT THAT DOES NOT CHANGE HIS LOVE AND GRACE FOR US. This is why we must share our "dirty" stories. *When you fall into sin, the only time you fail is when you don't receive His forgiveness and forgive yourself.*

> This is the message we have heard from Him and announce to you, that God is Light, and in Him there is no darkness at all. If we say that we have fellowship with Him and *yet* walk in the darkness, we lie and do not practice the truth; but if we walk in the Light as He Himself is in the Light, we have fellowship with one another, and the blood of Jesus His Son cleanses us from all sin. If we say that we have no sin, we are deceiving ourselves and the truth is not in us. If we confess our sins, He is faithful and righteous to forgive us our sins and to cleanse us from all unrighteousness. If we say that we have not sinned, we make Him a liar and His word is not in us.
> —1 John 1:5-10 NASB

There is a God that has seen beyond our sin before we were born. There is a God that still searches us to show us our ways so they we can shine more like Him. We receive Jesus to reflect the character of the Father.

We believe the gospel by faith, but we need to share the gospel along with our stories by faith as well. Salvation was free, Justification is by faith, and Sanctification is work through the Holy Spirit enabling us to live a holy life separate from the world. Glorification is coming! We will take off this dirty flesh one day.

> Now I say this, brethren, that flesh and blood cannot inherit the kingdom of God; nor does the perishable inherit the imperishable. Behold, I tell you a mystery; we will not all sleep, but we will all be changed, in a moment, in the twinkling of an eye, at the last trumpet; for the trumpet will sound, and the dead will be raised imperishable, and we will be changed. For this perishable must put on the imperishable, and this mortal must put on immortality. But when this perishable will have put on the imperishable, and this mortal will have put on immortality, then will come about the saying that is written, "DEATH IS SWALLOWED UP in victory. "O DEATH, WHERE IS YOUR VICTORY? O DEATH, WHERE IS YOUR STING?" The sting of death is sin, and the power of sin is the law; but thanks be to God, who gives us the victory through our Lord Jesus Christ. Therefore, my beloved brethren, be steadfast, immovable, always abounding in the work of the Lord, knowing that your toil is not *in* vain in the Lord.
>
> —1 Corinthians 15:50-58 NASB

There will be a day when we will never have to share our "dirty" stories ever again because we will be like Him.

> See how great a love the Father has bestowed on us, that we would be called children of God; and *such* we are. For this reason the world does not know us, because it did not know Him. Beloved, now we are children of God, and it has not appeared as yet what we will be. We know that when He appears, we will be like Him, because we will see Him just as He is. And everyone who has this hope *fixed* on Him purifies himself, just as He is pure. Everyone who practices sin also practices lawlessness; and sin is lawlessness.
>
> —1 John 3:1-4 NASB

## POUR LiKE NEVER BEFORE

Never forget Mary poured out worship from an authentic place. She poured out her passion for *His pursuit* of her. She didn't feel worthy of His love and forgiveness, but it humbled her to honor Him. We would not be a worthy recipient of the Love of God without Christ. Whatever may seem costly to us we must give Him our worth-ship. How much is Jesus worth to you? Break open the box of your heart and pour it out every chance you get. Think back over your life and just start pouring out your worship to God for His love, grace, and forgiveness. Let nothing or no one hinder you from pouring out your life. Pour at home! Pour on your job! Pour at school! Pour with your family! Pour in your church! Pour in your community! Pour in your car! POUR LIKE NEVER BEFORE! We must pour because God poured:

> And hope does not disappoint, because the love of God has been poured out within our hearts through the Holy Spirit who was given to us. For while we were still helpless, at the right time Christ died for the ungodly.
>
> —Romans 5:5-6 NASB

Paul poured until there was no more!

> But even if I am being poured out as a drink offering upon the sacrifice and service of your faith, I rejoice and share my joy with you all.
>
> —Philippians 2:17 NASB

> For I am already being poured out as a drink offering, and the time of my departure has come. I have fought the good fight, I have finished the course, I have kept the faith; in the future there is laid up for me the crown of righteousness, which the Lord, the righteous Judge, will award to me on that day; and not only to me, but also to all who have loved His appearing.
>
> —2 Timothy 4:6-8 NASB

God poured, Jesus poured, The Holy Spirit poured, Mary poured, Paul poured, and We need to pour. Pour like never before! Pour from your place of Repentance! Pour from your place of Restoration. Pour from your place of Redemption. Pour out Love! Pour out Grace! Pour out Forgiveness! Pour out Truth! Pour out Joy! Pour out Peace! Pour out Mercy! Pour out Faith! Pour out Hope! Pour out of Holiness! For the blood of Jesus Christ has Rescued and Redeemed us from every *dirty place*, the Holy Spirit of God has covered the *distance* to reach us, and God the Father brought us out of the *dark place* to make us His children. LET HIS LIMITLESS LOVE BE THE SOURCE THAT FILLS YOUR SOUL. Let His WORD be the nourishment that feeds your being. Let His GRACE be the goodness that leads you to repentance. Let His TRUTH be the Way that leads you to Life. POUR LIKE NEVER BEFORE THEN ASK GOD FOR MORE, SO HIS LOVE IS LAVISHED UPON THE LIVES OF ALL WE ENCOUNTER!

DON'T FORGET TO **TELL YOUR STORY** EVERYWHERE THE GOSPEL OF JESUS CHRIST IS PREACHED! **NO ONE IS TOO DIRTY FOR GOD'S LOVE!**

We loved you so much that we shared with you **not only God's Good News but our own lives, too.**

—1 Thessalonians 2:8 NLT

And they overcame him because of the blood of the Lamb and **because of the word of their testimony**, and they did not love their life even when faced with death.

—Revelation 12:11 NASB

GOD LOVES YOU FROM THE INSIDE OUT!

Soli Gloria Deo

# END NOTES

As I closed the writing of the first draft of *Dirty Christianity*, I read A. W. Tozer's, *Knowledge of the Holy* for the first time. I came to the conclusion that God will continue to raise up voices with a clarion call to bring the Christian Church back to the foundation of faith of why Jesus Christ died and resurrected. As these same issues occurred in the 20th century church and prior, it is a confirmation of my call to be one of the voices that desire believers and unbelievers to experientially know our Holy and Loving God we serve. I agree with Tozer, *"The most important thing a Christian can do is to think rightly about God."* We must come to know God intimately in all His infinite attributes so that true healing can take place. May the awakening come soon Lord!

If you, or anyone you know has dealt with or is currently dealing with any form of abuse (sexual, emotional, physical, or spiritual) please purchase the book and workbook *Mending the Soul* by Dr. Steven and

Celestia Tracy. If you live in Phoenix or the surrounding cities there are small groups around the valley where you can begin your healing process. Go to www.mendingthesoul.org for more information.

I would recommend you download every song listed in this book to remind you of the awesome Love the Father has for us, if they are not already in your worship music library. All songs can be downloaded from iTunes or any music media platform. All song lyrics listed are the intellectual copy written property of the writers and publishers.

To download my latest album *Follow After Love* go to www.bigwo.com or iTunes. Give it as a gift to a young person or someone in your circle of influence.

For more information about Church of The Remnant, Phoenix, Arizona go to www.remnantmovement.com

# BOOK REFERENCES

*Mending the Soul: Understanding Healing and Abuse* (book and workbook) by Dr. Steven and Celestia Tracy. ISBN-10: 0310259711 / ISBN-13: 978-0310259718

*Crazy Love: Overwhelmed by a Relentless God* by Francis Chan. ISBN: 1434768511 / ISBN-13: 978-1434768513

*The Knowledge of the Holy: The Attributes of God: Their Meaning in the Christian Life* by A. W. Tozer. ISBN 10: 0060684127 / ISBN 13: 9780060684129

*Legalism is Lethal in the Spiritual Life* by Dr. Fred Chay. Available at www.graceline.net

*Total Forgiveness* by R. T. Kendall. ISBN-10: 1599791765 / ISBN-13: 9781599791760

# BiBLiOGRAPHY

Tracy, Steven R. Mending the Soul: Understanding Healing and Abuse. Grand Rapids: Zondervan, 2005

Chan, Francis. Crazy Love: Overwhelmed by a Relentless God. Colorado Springs: David C. Cook, 2008.

Tozer, A. W. The Knowledge of the Holy: The Attributes of God: Their Meaning in the Christian Life. San Francisco: HarperCollins, 1961.

Chay, Fred. Legalism is Lethal in the Spiritual Life. Phoenix: Grace Line, Inc., 2009.

Kendall, R. T. Total Forgiveness. Lake Mary: Charisma House, 2002.

# ACKNOWLEDGEMENTS

I want to acknowledge and thank so many people that have poured into my life over the years in my spiritual journey.

First, I would like to thank my dad, (Dr. Warren H. Stewart, Sr.) and my mom (Serena M. Stewart) for training me up in the way that I should go and seeing the tangible evidence that I have not departed from it (Proverbs 22:6). Dad, you were my first pastor and mom you were my first Sunday school teacher. Thank you for our upbringing despite all the trials we have gone through as a family. You taught us how to pray, read scripture, preach and serve in holistic ministry. The foundation of faith was laid and the seeds of righteousness are producing fruit. May love, grace, forgiveness and healing be true realities for our family for generations to come. I LOVE YOU ALL!

I want to thank my Uncle Tony and Aunt Jackie, (Pastor Anthony W. Green and Bishop Dr. Jackie L. Green) for investing so much time into my life and call, which caused me to grow in the confidence of being authentically me. You both helped pull out every creative gift that God has placed in me. You wouldn't take no for an answer when I was fearful and have stirred tremendous spiritual development in my life, family and ministry. Much of who I am in the ministry is because of your great investment. I stand on your shoulders. I LOVE YOU TWO!

Miss Rita, (Rev. MarQuerita Story) I thank you for being the realest woman of God I know. I have talked to you about any and everything in my life and ministry and you have never judged me. You have always given me truth, transparency and always pushed me to my purpose when I was down on myself. Your voice has been so valuable to my life and destiny. I LOVE YOU DEARLY!

To Pastor Brenda Davis, thank you for always keeping it real with me when I was making mistakes and didn't care about the consequences. You told me the truth when no one was watching. I miss you and will see you when I get to heaven. I LOVE YOU!

To Pastor CJ Blair you were the last piece in my purpose to push me out of the religious and traditional "Matrix" we call church. You are proof of those whom God can radically change through the Power of the Gospel and the Holy Spirit. Thank you for always keeping it "100" and telling me to Preach the Gospel! REMNANT exists because of our connection and your conviction to Come Our From Among Them. I LOVE YOU MAN!

To Pastor C. L. Mitchell, thank you for being such a great mentor, pastor, confidant, and friend. Because of your investment, my personal life and ministry has grown deeper in maturity and responsibility as a husband, father, and pastor. Thank you for causing me to be a great thinker of theology and searcher of the Scriptures. I LOVE YOU SIR!

To Dr. Steve Tracy, thank you for being such a kind, compassionate and heartfelt man of God. Yes, you are my professor and new mentor, but you and your wife's heart's are for the broken to be healed, which further confirms what God has called my wife and I to do. I am fortunate to be connected with people that really walk with those in their journey of healing when most Christians wouldn't deal with the stark reality of pain. You two are truly examples of the LOVE OF GOD. You are treasures to the body of Christ. I am grateful for you! I LOVE YOU BOTH!

Francis Chan, thank you for being an inspiration. We may never meet again, but I want to thank you for writing *Crazy Love* and walking by faith to discover the destiny that God has drawn out for you. I LOVE YOU TOO!

To Bryan, my friend and brother, thank you for always telling me that DADDY LOVES ME. Our Father uses you at the most opportune times to bless me with what we often seem to forget, but so desperately need to hear. I LOVE YOU BRO!

There are countless others and I can't name you all, but thank you to all the friends, mentors, pastors, men, and women of God who have trained, taught, poured, and preached into my life the rich mercies of God. I stand today because of your investment. I LOVE YOU ALL!